Safety in the Salon

A Guide for Hairdressing and Beauty Professionals

Elaine Almond

B.Sc.(Hons.), Cert.Ed., C.Biol., M.I.Biol.

MACMILLAN

First published by Stanley Thornes (Publishers) Ltd 1986
Fully revised and updated edition published in 1998 by
MACMILLAN PRESS LTD
Houndmills, Basingstoke, Hampshire RG21 6XS
and London
Companies and representatives throughout the world

ISBN 0–333–73006–2

A catalogue record for this book is available from the British Library.

This book is printed on paper suitable for recycling and made from fully managed and sustained forest sources.

Original design by Wendi Watson

10   9   8   7   6   5   4   3   2   1
07   06   05   04   03   02   01   00   99   98

Typeset by Tek-Art, Croydon, Surrey
Printed in Hong Kong

Contents

Contents

Foreword

I have a friend who works for a well known local company. Each week he would deposit that week's takings in the bank. One day he was pushed from the back and the bag that contained the takings was ripped from his hands. He never knew what had hit him and within seconds the robber had sped away.

Luckily he was not hurt too badly; only his pride! It was only when the police interviewed him that he realised that he was a suspect. The robber was never found. My friend recovered from his injuries and he managed to convince his employer and the police that he was an innocent victim.

The moral? Protect your staff, safeguard your money, assess the risks and plan accordingly. This excellent book will help you plan so you never have to tell a story like this.

Alan Goldsbro
Chief Executive, Hairdressing Training Board

Hairdressing Training Board/Macmillan Series

Related Macmillan titles

Manicure, Pedicure and Advanced Nail Techniques,
by Elaine Almond

The Nail File, by Leo Palladino and June Hunt

Start Hairdressing! – The Official Guide to Level 1,
by Martin Green and Leo Palladino

Hairdressing: The Foundations – The Official Guide to Level 2,
by Leo Palladino

Professional Hairdressing – The Official Guide to Level 3,
by Martin Green, Lesley Kimber and Leo Palladino

Beauty Therapy – The Foundations,
by Lorraine Nordmann

The Complete Make-up Artist: Working in Film, Television and Theatre,
by Penny Delamar

Science and the Beauty Business:
The Science of Cosmetics, and
The Beauty Salon and its Equipment,
both by John V. Simmons

Patrick Cameron: Dressing Long Hair,
by Patrick Cameron and Jacki Wadeson

Mahogany: Steps to Cutting, Colouring and Finishing Hair,
by Martin Gannon and Richard Thompson

The World of Hair: A Scientific Companion,
by John Gray

African-Caribbean Hairdressing,
by Sandra Gittens

The Art of Hair Colouring,
by David Adams and Jacki Wadeson

Hairdressing Training Board/Macmillan Series
Series Standing Order 0–333–69338–8

You can receive future titles in this series as they are published by placing a standing order. Please contact your bookseller or, in case of difficulty, write to us at the address below with your name and address, the title of the series and the ISBN quoted above.

Customer Services Department, Macmillan Distribution Ltd
Houndmills, Basingstoke, Hampshire RG21 6XS, England

Acknowledgements

The author would like to thank the following people for their help in the preparation of this book: Michael G. Almond, Mastercraftsman Hairdresser, for his help and advice with compiling the sections on hairdressing; June Armstrong from the Lancashire Constabulary Police Headquarters at Hutton, Lancashire, for her help and advice with compiling the section on personal safety and security; the Fire Prevention Department at the Fire Station, Chorley; the members of the Environmental Health Department at Chorley Borough Council Offices, Lancashire; and Pamela Linforth and Lawrence Green of Ellisons, Coventry, both of whom have always been generous with their assistance and advice.

In addition, the author and publisher would like to thank the following for providing pictures for the book: BaByliss, Bellitas, BLM Health, Body Guard Security Co. Ltd, Caress Ear Piercing, Carlton, Chubb Fire Ltd, Computill Ltd, Depilex, Dr M. H. Beck (Consultant Dermatologist, Bradford Royal Infirmary), Ellisons, Frank Pegg (Volumatic), Helionova, Ian Flanders, John V. Simmons, L'Oréal, Mahogany, Martin Green (Head Quarters), National Westminster Bank, Neville Daniel, S. Lewis, Sorisa, Wella.

Every effort has been made to trace all copyright holders, but if any have been inadvertently overlooked the publishers will be pleased to make the necessary arrangements at the first opportunity.

Introduction

Hairdressing and beauty therapy involve close liaison with the public. This unavoidable contact places both hairdresser and beauty therapist at risk from violence or aggression, while many of the treatments carried out in their working environments can be potentially dangerous due to the equipment and chemicals involved.

Large numbers of people, including the staff, enter hairdressing and beauty salons each week. It is inevitable that a small percentage of these people will, at some time, act in an aggressive or violent manner, have an accident, or be taken ill while on the premises. Such incidents require prompt thinking and action on the part of the hairdresser or therapist involved if the danger or damage is to be minimised and controlled.

A large part of this book describes sensible working practices developed over 55 years of practical experience. Many of these practices have now been formalised in laws and regulations which must be adhered to.

It is with all these factors in mind that this book has been written. It is arranged in four parts for ease of reference.

Part One is concerned with **personal safety and security.** Personal safety is, of necessity, at the centre of media attention at the moment. Unfortunately, open public contact increasingly coincides with vulnerability and exposure to verbal, mental or physical abuse. This part explores the sources of such problems, as well as giving guidelines on how to avoid dangerous situations. Suggestions are given on how to behave in hazardous situations to minimise their effects. Everything from alcohol abuse to sexual harassment is included, with special sections on safety for mobile workers and job interviewees.

Part Two is concerned with **accident prevention and safety** in the salon. For ease of access to the information, this part is further subdivided into three sections, covering situations:

1 in **general,** i.e. common to all hair, nail, health and beauty therapy salons. Simple but thorough coverage of the rules and regulations affecting these industries is included here
2 specific to **beauty, nail and health** businesses
3 specific to **hairdressing** salons.

Each situation or treatment is listed in alphabetical order within each section, setting out the potential dangers involved, with suggestions on how to avoid or minimise these dangers. Contraindications to the application of each specific treatment are also included.

Part Three lists alphabetically each **accident or illness** that may arise in hairdressing and beauty salons. A description of the symptoms is followed in each case by the appropriate **first aid** treatment to be administered according to the current (1996) First Aid at Work guidelines.

Part Four deals with the **legal requirements** for every workplace to have adequate and suitable **first-aid equipment**, and an **appointed person** who is responsible for:

- maintaining the first-aid equipment
- the provision of first aid on the premises – Health and Safety (First Aid) Regulations 1981, updated 1996
- the correct recording and reporting of accidents (RIDDOR).

This part of the book also contains suggestions for additional items to be kept with the first-aid box to help the hairdresser and therapist deal quickly and effectively with any accident or emergency that may arise.

Together, these four parts contain all the information hair and beauty professionals need to know in order to keep themselves, their staff and their clients **safe in the salon.**

PART ONE

Personal safety and security

Personal safety and security

The hairdressing and beauty therapy professions involve close contact with the public, and increasingly this contact can lead to vulnerability and exposure to harm. Every day the news seems to carry reports of petty theft, robbery, fraud, breaking and entering, violence, stalking, harassment, rape, murder, road rage and acts of aggression due to alcohol, drugs or stress. The danger cannot be ignored, but it can be reduced by being aware of the risks involved, taking adequate precautions to guard against danger, and acting in appropriate ways to minimise an incident should one occur.

Sources of harm

Harm can be verbal, mental or physical, and can come from many sources.

RECEPTION AND IN WORK

- unhappy clients or relatives/friends of clients wanting amends to be made for what they see as unsatisfactory service
- people under the influence of drink or drugs, or mentally unstable characters attending for prebooked appointments or demanding appointments 'now'.
- sexual harassment
- stealing, from petty theft to aggravated burglary with use of violence
- attack when on your own in the premises

TELEPHONE

- unhappy or dissatisfied clients, sometimes leading to verbal threats
- sexual harassment – repeated unwanted calls
- shocking, threatening, verbally abusive or sexually suggestive telephone calls
- vindictive ex-members of staff

FELLOW STAFF MEMBERS

- bullying, intimidation, jealousy, gossiping, unfair booking, aggressive competition and poaching of clients, constructive dismissal
- drug and alcohol abuse among fellow members of staff.
- sexual harassment
- stealing from workmates

OUTSIDE THE WORK PREMISES

- attack when travelling to and from work
- attack when carrying out banking activities for the salon
- attack when carrying out mobile work, both while travelling or when in someone's house
- attack when attending a job interview

Avoidance of harm

The owner or manager of the business and premises can do a great deal to make the working environment and conditions safe and avoid potentially harmful situations arising.

THE RECEPTION DESK

Picture a cluttered reception desk next to the entrance, with charity boxes and a telephone on the top, the appointment book and till in full view and easily accessible, and the client coat-hanging area tucked away behind the desk, not to mention retail sales goods stacked on the desk and adjacent open shelving. The picture is probably not difficult to imagine as most reception desks in small hair and beauty salons look like this.

Now picture a naughty child or a drug addict dashing in off the street, snatching a charity box or expensive retail item and running away; a thief waiting until the shop is empty at lunchtime, then walking in through the unlocked door and walking

Neville Daniel

out with the till; a verbally abusive drunk standing at the desk demanding an appointment *now* because they can see, no matter how much you protest, that the appointment book is empty and you have room to fit them in; a client going to get their own coat but taking a better one instead, or casually taking a few notes from the improperly closed till; and an unaccompanied person, perhaps waiting for an appointment or having been given permission to use the telephone, leaning across the desk to help themselves to the contents of the till. All these things happen and are easily avoidable.

DESIGN OF THE SALON AND RECEPTION AREA

- The reception desk should be placed as far away from the entrance as salon design will allow.
- The desk should be wide. It should be high on the clients' side so that they cannot see, reach or jump over it. The till, appointment book and computer should be kept lower down and hidden on the staff side. A safety **panic button** linked to an alarm or preferably the local police station should be within easy reach of staff, but concealed from clients, for use in case of serious incidents.
- Clients' coats should be kept in a separate cloakroom area away from the till and retail areas. This should be accessed by staff only so that clients do not inadvertently or purposefully take the wrong coat.
- Displays of retail stock should be kept behind locked laminated glass doors, or all displays made of empty boxes only and signs displayed to inform clients of this fact.

- Signs can also be displayed encouraging the use of cheques or credit cards for payment, and advising clients that very little cash is kept in the till at any one time.

TIP BOX

If you have a charity box in your salon, keep it out of sight of the door and bolted to the wall to prevent it being stolen. Avoid clutter, confusion and added risk of theft by only having one.

- Clients should have their own pay telephone situated away from the desk, preferably bolted to the wall.
- The salon telephone is best bolted to the wall behind the reception desk. Important telephone numbers, e.g. police, fire brigade, ambulance and hospital, should be clearly displayed next to this telephone.
- The reception desk and any activities taking place there should be clearly visible from all other parts of the salon. This can be achieved by using a system of convex or plain mirrors suitably arranged, or a closed-circuit TV system.

SALON SECURITY

Break-ins to closed premises can be largely prevented by the use of adequate precautionary measures such as suitable locks (insurance recommended and at least to British Standard 3621 – look for the Kitemark), burglar alarms, security lighting, closed-circuit TV, laminated glass windows and other precautionary measures.

Theft from premises during opening hours can be minimised by the use of equipment such as panic buttons, convex mirrors and closed-circuit TV, as well as the sensible working procedures and salon design already mentioned.

As these crime prevention methods are changing and improving all the time, and vary so much depending on the structure of the premises concerned, professional advice must be sought. Approach your local police station first and ask to speak to the Crime Prevention Officer (CPO). Different forces have different policies regarding crime prevention. Often the CPO will visit your premises free of charge if requested and give specific advice about windows, doors, and structural defence against crime. As regards the design, installation and maintenance of an alarm system, the CPO will supply you with the names and addresses of the relevant recognised associations and professional bodies, e.g. NACOSS or BSIA, who will in turn be able to supply you with the names and addresses of local reputable advisers and installers. Alternatively, your insurance company may insist that you use someone supplied or recommended by them, so always contact them first. *Never* simply choose an installer from an advert or telephone listing.

Having taken advice from the CPO and obtained a list of reputable alarm installation firms, ask for at least *three* independent price quotations for any work to be carried out, thus getting three sets of installation ideas as well as prices. If in doubt as to which is the best installation design, do not hesitate to return to your local CPO for further advice and guidance. The most expensive and complicated state-of-the-art system may not be the most efficient for your purposes. Be guided by the CPO.

Once you have decided on a suitable design, go back to the three firms and ask for requotes for exactly what you want installed. Choosing the company is as important as choosing the system. Make sure you select a company which can give a prompt call-out service in case of a fault, as well as a reliable annual service and maintenance contract. Can the system be maintained by other companies if the installing company closes down for any reason?

TIP BOX

Choose a burglar alarm installer that is a member of one of the professional bodies, e.g. NACOSS or BSIA. This will tell you that the company has met the stringent standards of membership. It also means that, if the installation is not up to standard, you can refer the problem to the professional body for investigation and rectification at no cost to yourself.

EMPLOYEE CRIME

Employee crime is not a problem anyone likes to think of as happening to them, but it is a fact of life

and sensible, balanced precautionary measures can to a large extent prevent its occurrence.

It is important to try to employ honest staff with stable backgrounds. Take time to hold an in-depth interview; consider having them in the salon to work with you for a trial period of, for example, a day; and *always* take up references.

During the interview, talk to them about your policies regarding staff security. Explain your security rules, making these few in number and therefore easy to uphold, but strictly enforced. State that a search clause is included in their terms of employment, i.e. any employee may be randomly searched when they leave the premises. Also make sure they understand that thieves are *always* prosecuted and that employee theft results in instant dismissal, high fines, payment of court costs, financial compensation for the loss to the employer, suspended or actual prison sentences, and the resultant personal consequences of a criminal record.

TIP BOX

Make sure employees know exactly what is expected of them. Keep security rules clear and consistent, and enforce them strictly.

All the above can be explained when reading the job description, terms of employment, or work contract with the employee. It is very important to have a fully comprehensive contract which works for your business, but also means that employees know exactly what the employer's work policies are and what duties and work responsibilities are expected of them. An initial agreement avoids mistakes, waste, poor standards of work, misunderstandings, ill feeling and dishonesty.

Show staff that you care for them. A caring employer (do not confuse being caring with being soft) will have fewer problems with employee crime. Be fair, look after your employees, and do not show favouritism. Most employees steal as a way of striking back at an uncaring organisation or at what they perceive to be the unfairness of life in general. Get the staff involved in the security of the salon; make them feel part of a team effort and wanted.

Unfortunately, honesty cannot be taken for granted, particularly from long-serving employees who are trusted and in a position to know how to bend the rules. Be aware that *anyone* can steal.

Dishonesty can come in many forms. Here are just some possibilities:

- taking a perm solution from the stock cupboard to do your mother's hair at home
- doing clients' treatments away from the salon and getting paid directly, thus depriving the salon of income (a salon should have a written policy regarding staff working away from the salon out of hours and make this part of the work contract)
- pocketing the correct payment money instead of ringing it into the till
- bringing friends or relatives into the salon for free treatments when the owner/manager is not there or not aware that a charge is not being made (checking the appointment book/potential takings against the actual takings in the till can pinpoint these latter two cheats)
- applying staff discounts to retail stock for the use of others
- taking sick leave when not ill
- getting paid for overtime not worked
- taking and keeping personal property belonging to fellow employees.

COUNTERFEIT CURRENCY, PLASTIC CARD AND CHEQUE BOOK FRAUD

Counterfeit currency

The law regarding counterfeit currency states:

1 You cannot make counterfeit money.
2 You cannot pass on counterfeit money if you have had counterfeits given to you, i.e. you cannot get rid of them to the next customer.
3 You cannot keep counterfeit money to show it to your friends or colleagues.

If you break any of the above three rules, the punishment can be up to 10 years in jail.

All counterfeit money must be handed in to the police and there is no compensation for people who have had fake notes passed on to them. All staff must therefore be trained to carefully examine every bank note before accepting it. The checks are as follows:

1 The silver thread woven into the paper has a dotted appearance on one side that is impossible to replicate accurately.
2 The water mark of the queen's head is an accurate representation – forgeries are often inked in and have a cartoon-like appearance.

3 The paper quality is high with a particular feel to it.
4 The print also has a feel to it that counterfeit notes cannot reproduce.
5 Two new features are the international copyright symbol in multicoloured ink on the bottom left of the front of the note, and the multicoloured number with digits of varying heights on the front left of the note.

Equipment purporting to check for counterfeit notes, e.g. ultra-violet and pens, is helpful but not foolproof.

Plastic cards

Staff need to be trained to check plastic cards for their **validity** as well as how to use them for money transactions. Below are some guidelines on how to do this.

1 Is the card still current?
2 Has it been signed in the required ball-point pen and not felt tip? Felt tip can cover up a previous signature.
3 Remove the card from its wallet – does it look and feel as it should? Is the signature strip smooth when you run your nail over it – not a strip of paper stuck over the original strip?
4 Get the customer to sign the voucher without seeing the card so they cannot copy the signature. Check that the signatures tally.
5 Always obtain authorisation from the card company after completion and signing of the sales voucher and use of the imprinter. Take the voucher and card with you and do it out of sight of the customer.
6 If the authorisation is refused, retain the card. Rewards are given for the retention of fraudulent cards and the prevention of fraudulent transactions.
7 If you feel the retention of the card or the discovery of the fraud will cause possible violent confrontation with the customer, call the police

A cheque guarantee/service card

while still out of sight and delay the transaction in some way until they arrive.

8   The processing copies of sales vouchers need to be banked as soon as possible. There is often considerable delay between the theft of a card and its discovery and notification.

Cheque books

As well as knowing how to take payment by cheque, staff need to know what to look for in case of fraud, e.g. a stolen cheque book. Below are some guidelines.

1   Never take cheques without guarantee cards, making the appropriate checks on the card as described above.
2   Does the sort code on the cheque correspond with that on the card?
3   If you have the slightest doubt about the signature, get the customer to sign the back of the cheque out of sight of any previous signature.
4   Never accept a cheque which has been defaced by alteration, smudging or black marks.
5   A member of staff must write the card number on the back of the cheque, not the customer. One digit difference will invalidate it.
6   If possible a second member of staff should be asked to doublecheck all details of the transaction, and both members should initial the back of the cheque so the transaction can be traced if necessary.
7   Traveller's cheques need to be backed up with positive identification, e.g. a passport.
8   Cheques need to be banked as soon as possible. There is often considerable delay between theft of a cheque book and its discovery.

Most local Chambers of Commerce or police stations have an early warning scheme. If you join

you will get a small notice to place in your window or at the reception desk, stating that police can be notified rapidly if shop theft, plastic card or cheque book fraud takes place. Such a deterrent is often the best way of dealing with fraudsters.

Criminals often watch to see how staff carry out transactions. If they see that the staff are well trained and carry out all the necessary checks efficiently, they will often leave you alone and go elsewhere where their job will be easier.

TIP BOX

If you are uneasy about the behaviour of any customer but cannot identify a cause, note down any relevant details, e.g. their car number plate if possible, or what they are wearing and look like. Do not rely on memory. Such details may prove useful later.

CASHING UP AND BANKING

Salon takings have to be cashed up and taken to the bank, and at all stages this can be potentially dangerous. Thieves watch for patterns of banking behaviour, e.g. taking money to the bank, collecting staff wages from the bank, or staff taking their wages to the bank. They will attack at the most vulnerable time for you and the most financially rewarding time for themselves. Again, you can lessen the probability of this happening by taking basic precautions.

*   Do not leave the reception area unattended during working hours. This applies at lunchtime too. Attend the desk or lock the doors.
*   Keep as little money on the premises or on your person as possible. Encourage payment of large amounts by cheque or credit card and advertise this fact. Enough money in the till to give change for a £50 note is sufficient. Keep extra notes which build up through the day in a strong, secure container (counter cache) which is bolted underneath or beside the till. By removing surplus notes from the till you reduce the temptations of both a cash snatch and employee theft.
*   When cashing up, make sure that all the clients have left the premises and all doors, front and back, are locked. Always cash up and make up

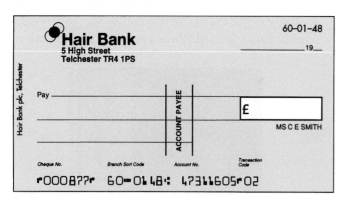

A cheque

Frank Pegg, Volumatic

Frank Pegg, Volumatic

A counter cache

Keep as little money in the till as possible

your head and under your coat. Your personal alarm should be readily to hand, *not* in the bottom of your bag. This method is most suitable for carrying small amounts of money covertly.

- An alternative school of thought recommends carrying money in a shoulder bag or briefcase with an automatic smoke and/or alarm device. The device is thrown at the attacker, thus

Frank Pegg, Volumatic

A briefcase with an automatic smoke alarm

till floats out of sight of passers-by, preferably in an office. Weighing machines which count notes and coins quickly are available to speed up the cashing-up process.

- If you have to move money from the till or counter cache to an office during working hours, do so in a secure manner using a special cash-carrying case.
- Bank frequently, every day or twice a day if the salon is busy, e.g. at Christmas time. Try to bank during bank opening hours if possible, as it is safer to carry out transactions inside the bank rather than outside at the bank booth. However, do use the night-safe facility if this is not possible. Do not take and keep quantities of money at home. This is inviting robbery, either on your way home or at home.
- Only the owner should have the responsibility of taking money to and from the bank. The Health and Safety at Work Regulations 1992 require employers to assess the risks to the safety of their employees of every job they do. Banking duties carry too much risk to be undertaken by employees – even by very senior, security-checked, sensible and trusted members of staff.
- Bank at different times; do not have a set routine.
- Consider having accounts with more than one bank, using each in an irregular pattern.
- If you go to the bank by car, park next to the bank or choose a bank with a drive-through facility. Do not use taxis or public transport.
- When carrying money on your person, keep it hidden next to you in a 'bum bag' or body belt, or a small, strong shoulderbag with the strap over

Frank Pegg, Volumatic

A security bag

hopefully keeping the cash carrier safe while maximising the chance of recovering the money. You can also carry money in a shoulder bag, which for added security has a wrist band attached to a chain. Such equipment is available from security shops.

- It is always recommended that two people travel together on banking journeys.
- Be aware of your surroundings and people around you, especially people jostling you. Walk down the middle of deserted pavements, face the oncoming traffic, be careful around concealed entrances and poorly lit areas, and avoid deserted places and car parks. Take care around bank cashpoints.
- If you think you are being followed, cross the road, turning as you do so to check behind you. If they cross, cross again, and again if necessary. Keep moving and head for a busy area, service station, café or other public facility. Go in, ask for help and telephone the police.
- If you get to a night-safe facility and find it jammed or blocked in any way (super glue is a favourite), move away immediately and return to somewhere safe, then call the police. This blocking is often a delaying manoeuvre on the part of thieves to keep you at the terminal long enough for them to attack you. This ploy is also used on car locks; if you experience it, move away from your car quickly and call the police.
- If you are threatened or attacked, a loud shout or activation of a personal alarm can often cause the attacker to run away. Shout a definite instruction to any passers-by, e.g. 'phone the police', as they are more likely to react to a specific command than to what they may see as an ambiguous situation in which they may not want to get involved. Be prepared to give up your money container if snatched. Carry a small amount of money and a phone card in another pocket to allow you to call for help or get home if no help is at hand.

All the above information and guidance refers to general banking safety for a small business, e.g. just the owner, or the owner with 1–4 staff. In bigger salons, larger amounts of money can be involved. Here your insurance company will often give explicit guidelines on how money has to be transported to the bank and how much can be carried at any one time. All salons, large and small, must check with their insurance company and comply with their recommendations.

For greater peace of mind, consider forming a group with other local shopkeepers to employ a cash in transit (CIT) security company (ask the CPO to recommend a reputable company). Once the money is handed over to them on your premises, it is no longer your responsibility.

OUTSIDE THE WORK PREMISES

- If travelling by car to and from work, park as close to work as possible in a well-lit area. Park in busy areas near carpark attendants or pay-and-display machines, *not* in isolated areas of the parking ground.
- Take extra care on dark mornings and nights during the winter months. Walk to and from your car with another person. Why not share the journey with a friend or colleague?
- If on reaching your car you find the lock blocked up in any way, e.g. with chewing gum or superglue, do not waste time but quickly move away to a safe area and call the police. It could be a delaying tactic, giving a person time to attack you.

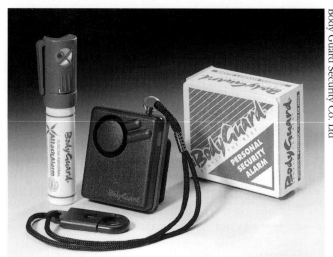

A personal alarm

Body Guard Security Co. Ltd

TIP BOX

Pay staff wages directly into their bank accounts so that you do not have to handle large amounts of money for wages, and they do not have to be responsible for large sums of money at work or on their way home.

Carry a personal alarm, e.g. a Suzy Lampugh Trust Alarm (address on page 12), to alert others in case of attack. Clip it on to your clothing – it cannot help you at the bottom of your handbag or briefcase!

MOBILE WORK

In mobile work expensive equipment and money are being transported around, so all the advice given in the above 'banking' and 'outside the work permises' sections applies, along with the points below.

If you are working outside the salon, make sure someone knows where you are going, and let them know if you change your plans. Contact them when you have arrived at your destination and/or when you arrive home so that they know you are safe. Going into other people's homes, especially when you do not know them, can carry considerable risk.

- Carry a mobile telephone with which to call for help should you get into difficulty or break down.
- Carry some small change and a phonecard in case there is an emergency and your phone is not working or stolen. Never accept lifts from strangers, or even taxis which pull up as they may be bogus. Carry the telephone number of a reputable taxi firm.
- Carry a personal alarm close to hand.
- Know where you are going and plan your route so you do not have to stop and ask for directions.
- Keep the windows and doors locked when in the car, especially when you have to stop at junctions and lights.
- Do not stop if you see an incident, accident or someone tries to flag you down. Continue on but report what you have seen at the next telephone, or use your mobile phone.
- If you think you are being followed, keep driving until you come to a busy place, e.g. a garage forecourt or a police, fire or ambulance station.

- If a car pulls alongside at lights or a junction and the occupants try to attract your attention, avoid eye contact and ignore them.
- If a car pulls alongside and forces you to stop, do not turn off your engine. If the driver leaves their car and approaches you, reverse as far as possible using your hazard lights and horn, keeping all doors and windows locked.
- Keep your car in good working condition. Carry extra petrol in a safety-approved petrol can and an automatic latex puncture aerosol to get you to the nearest garage.
- Be a member of one of the professional breakdown organisations and take their advice on a suitable burglar alarm system. If you break down and phone for help, tell them if you are a single woman or person on your own.
- A notice saying HELP CALL POLICE should be carried in the car. It can be displayed in the window towards traffic travelling in the same direction as yourself if the need arises. These notices are sometimes available free of charge from your local police headquarters.
- Take care to place any valuable items in the car out of sight, e.g. in the boot/trunk, when leaving it unattended.
- If you have to make a number of journeys to the car to get your equipment for working with, lock the car between visits. Otherwise a passer-by could reach in and steal something, or even steal the car.
- If you break down on a motorway, use your hazard lights and stop as far to the left on the hard shoulder and as near to an emergency telephone as possible. Use the front passenger door to leave the car, and lock all doors except this one. (Do not lock the doors if the car has central locking.) Keep to the inside of the hard shoulder when going to the phone and make sure that the emergency services know that you are on your own. Return to your car and wait on the embankment, not in your car. If you must wait in the car due to feeling threatened, wait in the front passenger seat with all the doors locked and return to the embankment when you feel the danger has passed.
- If you cannot get to the phone, the phone is out of order, or you feel unsafe leaving your car, place your HELP CALL POLICE poster in the rear window and stay with your car until help arrives. Police vehicles make frequent patrols.
- Completely trust only uniformed police officers.

Although most other people are trustworthy, you may prefer to talk with them through locked doors and a partially opened window.

- Never attempt repairs, e.g. changing a wheel, on the offside (motorway side) of your car.

For further information on mobile work, see page 38.

JOB INTERVIEWS

- Carefully check that job adverts are legitimate, e.g. the address/company really exists, or the agent has good credentials.
- If you are going through an agency, ensure that the agency checks out its clients, visits the employer's premises and provides detailed job descriptions. This is especially important when applying for a job abroad.

> **TIP BOX**
>
> Find out as much as possible about a potential employer in advance – it will provide you with useful information for the interview and help you to ensure the employer is genuine.

- Try to make sure that interviews take place at the office/premises of the employer or agency. If for any reason they are held elsewhere, make sure it is in a public place, or ask to take a friend along. If the interview is being held in a hotel, check with the hotel management that the firm involved is holding legitimate recruitment sessions there. Check that another person, e.g. a receptionist, will be present, or ask to take a friend along. (Note: the interviewer is also vulnerable to attack or false allegations of unfit behaviour from the interviewee if the interview is unchaperoned.)
- If the interview is outside working hours, ask someone to meet you at a specified time, and tell the interviewer that you are being met.
- Always make sure that someone knows you are going for an interview and at what time you expect to return.
- During an interview, keep the conversation away from personal subjects which bear no relation to the job, and never continue the interview over into a social occasion, e.g. drinks or dinner.
- Never accept a lift home from the interviewer; make your own prior arrangements.

> **TIP BOX**
>
> If you are going abroad for a job, take an emergency fund of money with you, sufficient to return home should you need to, and never part with your passport, no matter what your employer or anyone says. Provide copies for the use of others. Check travel and accommodation arrangements directly by phone or letter before you go, and ensure that key people, e.g. parents, relatives or close friends, know your contact details. Get as much information as possible about your employer and the work you will be expected to do, talking to current or prior employees if possible. If in doubt, do not accept the job.

How to behave in a potentially harmful situation

Avoidance of harm in a situation which is already in progress is often (but not always) due to how the person behaves and manages the situation.

People usually become abusive, aggressive or violent only if they are not getting what they want, i.e. if they feel aggrieved in some way. Examples of this could be not getting an appointment, being dissatisfied with the work carried out, or feeling that not enough attention or care is being given. If you work in a service industry, the ethic of 'the customer is always right' must hold true at all times.

Computill Ltd

The customer is always right

AVOIDANCE

The best way to prevent a violent or unpleasant situation is to avoid it.

- If something has gone wrong, do not deny it – own up to it and do everything in your power to put it right. Do not make a stand on false principles or pride, or hide behind authority, status or technical jargon.
- If the customer does not like what you are doing, change it. They are paying your wages. They deserve value and satisfaction for their money.

WARNING SIGNS

Sometimes a client's anger can be due to a frustrating situation occurring in their lives which is totally unrelated to the salon.

- Look for warning signs that all is not well. People seldom become violent without prior warning, for example signs of agitation; using aggressive or short, sharp clipped words; facial tightness and tension or change of colour.
- If warning signs occur, take steps to stop the incident from escalating. Never become aggressive yourself or use aggressive movements, e.g. putting your hands on your hips, folding your arms, wagging your finger or raising your arms.
- Never place a hand on someone who is angry, and keep your distance a protective arm's length or more away.
- Stay calm and speak slowly, clearly and gently, trying to talk things through as reasonable adults. Do not become drawn into an argument. This is not always easy as it is the nature of aggression to incite responding aggression in the recipient.

TALKING A SITUATION DOWN

Defuse the situation by talking the person down. A useful guide to doing this is summed up by the initials **LEAP**.

- **Listen** to the person and really look as if you are listening.
- **Empathise** with the way they feel. Imagine being in a similar situation yourself.
- **Ask questions** to gain an understanding of the problem and allow them to talk.
- **Paraphrase** back to them what they are saying to show that you are understanding the situation.

If the incident is in any way your fault, and sometimes even if it isn't, put the problem right. Ask the person what they want to make them feel better and do it. If they do not know, then suggest something. Make efforts to calm and defuse the situation.

Often the person is simply angry and needs to 'let off steam'. Let them talk themselves out. Here, the listening skills detailed above (LEAP) are invaluable. Most colleges of further education run basic Level One Listening Skills courses (approximately 25 hours) for people working with the public. Attend one if possible. Assertiveness training skills are also useful here.

PROTECT YOURSELF

Avoidance of a problem and talking down anger are the two main approaches to dealing with a potentially harmful situation. However, if the situation continues to escalate despite all the calming actions taken so far, you must protect yourself:

- Keep at least an arm's length away from the person so that you can see their body and be aware of any violent move towards you.
- Do not allow yourself to be trapped in a corner.
- Carry a personal attack alarm and be prepared to use it in such a situation. The noise may just shock the person into stopping, but it will also warn others that you are in trouble. The salon may also have a personal safety alarm button under the reception desk which will be linked to a salon alarm and possibly directly to the police station. Make sure you know where this is and how it works.

TIP BOX

No matter how aggravating a customer is being, do not be drawn into an argument. Try to calm a situation by talking to them and showing that you understand their needs. This way, you may avoid a difficult situation escalating out of control.

All this information can be adapted for use in situations outside the salon, e.g. a street incident or problems when doing mobile work. Avoidance is always the first step. If someone attempts to rob you, let them take the money. Acquiesce, do not antagonise. Remember the four stages:

1 **Avoid** the situation as far as possible by being aware, careful, or acquiescing.
2 Look for **warning signs** of a situation developing.
3 Try to **talk down** an incident – listen, empathise, ask questions, paraphrase back (LEAP).
4 **Protect yourself**.

Further information can be obtained from The Suzy Lampugh Trust, 14 East Sheen Avenue, London SW14 8AS. Telephone 0181 392 1839. Send a stamped addressed envelope for literature. Your local police CPO may also have booklets and organise courses on personal safety.

TIP BOX

If you are or have been a victim of crime in any way and are suffering mentally because of this, Victim Support offers counselling free of charge and can be contacted directly (the number is in the telephone directory) or through your local police station.

Armed robbery

To minimise the probability of an armed robbery occurring, make it known that the cash in the till and on the premises is kept to a minimum at any one time. Display a sign at reception stating this fact. Encourage payment by cheque or credit card instead of cash, bank frequently and pay staff wages directly into their accounts from your bank. Stay alert and report suspicious activity before it develops into trouble.

In the event of an armed attack:

- Do not panic. This can provoke shooting. The best way to avoid panic is by having had sufficient prior staff training in what to do in the event of such an attack.
- Follow the armed person's orders to the letter quickly. The sooner the confrontation is over the better. Do not argue; show extreme fear, panic, hostility or anger; hesitate; or try to talk

them out of the attack. This will not work and may antagonise them into shooting.

- Warn the robber quickly about possible surprises, e.g. someone in the staffroom who may reappear suddenly and unexpectedly, or the fact that you have to reach under the counter for a bag. A nervous robber could be startled into shooting by an unexpected occurrence.
- Try to observe the robber for future identification, but do not be too obvious. When they have left, write down these details and more if possible, e.g. number plate, make, model and colour of the car; escape route; clothes, hair and skin colour, height, gender, etc.
- Ask any witnesses to wait for the police.
- Close the salon or, at the very least, cordon off areas the robber might have touched for the police to inspect.

Armed robbery is a very traumatic experience and follow-up counselling will often be necessary for the people involved. Individual and group staff meetings after the event can allow those involved to talk about their unpleasant experience and come to terms with their fears and feelings.

TIP BOX

In the event of an armed robbery, never try to fight the aggressor – the money is not worth the risk to your life, and it should be recoverable through your insurance policy.

Bomb incidents

Unfortunately, all businesses now have to consider the possibility of a bomb incident occurring. This could be a telephone call threatening a bomb incident or informing you that a bomb is on your premises; a bomb in the post; a vehicle bomb parked near your premises; a bomb left inside your premises in a bag or other container; an incendiary (e.g. petrol) bomb thrown or brought into your premises; or a suicidal person with a bomb inside your premises.

The use of bombs is usually political, but other reasons could be racial or religious protests;

blackmail or intimidation; revenge or grudge vandalism; or as a diversion for other criminal activity occurring nearby.

Firstly, you must analyse the risk of such an incident occurring to you or your premises. You may be at risk for any of the reasons already given; you may be situated in a high-risk area, e.g. next to a bank, hotel, public building or armed forces recruitment office; or you may have one or more clients who are in a high-risk category.

Secondly you must plan for a possible bomb incident and train your staff thoroughly so that they know what to do if such an incident occurs. Appoint deputies in case of staff absence. Thorough training prevents panic and minimises accidents and damage.

Preventative measures include good salon security (see page 3) to prevent access by the bomber when the salon is closed; and staff being alert at all times for suspicious objects, vehicles and people inside and outside the premises. Laminated glass, heavy net curtains, or a special thin polyester film fixed to the inside of your windows will minimise damage from flying glass in the event of an explosion.

Have one place in the salon where clients leave their shopping bags and coats, and check that this is empty at the end of the day. This way suspicious objects are less likely to come into the salon and are easily spotted if they do. Keep the salon tidy and rubbish-free so that unusual items are rapidly seen.

If your salon is inside a shopping centre, find out from the police CPO what will happen if there is a local threat. Who will notify you, the police or the shopping centre co-ordinator? Is there an established contingency plan? Who will search the premises? Where is a safe place to evacuate to? Bear in mind that although 200 metres is considered a safe distance for fire evacuation, bomb threats need an evacuation distance of 400 metres. Work out your evacuation procedure according to this information.

Make sure that your local police station has the name and address of a keyholder to your premises in case they need to gain access.

If you think you have a suspect package in the salon, do not touch it or attempt to have a good look. Move all the people away and call the police. Place an identifying marker next to it, e.g. a piece of dayglow card or a handkerchief, to identify its position to the police when they arrive. Bombs can be in plastic bags, cardboard boxes, thermos flasks,

wastepaper bins, and audio or video cassettes. Look for anything which does not seem right or is out of place.

Watch out for warning signs of a postal bomb – be careful if a package smells of marzipan, has grease on the outside, is heavy for its size or has too many stamps, for example. Put it down gently, preferably in an isolated room, but do not waste time; walk away from it and clear the area of people; sound the alarm or call the police.

TIP BOX

If your building has alarms, remember that bomb alarms have a different sound to fire alarms to allow for the different evacuation procedures. Make sure you recognise them.

If you receive a telephone bomb threat, obtain as much information as possible and try to record the exact wording of the caller. Keep a checklist of information required next to the phone to help you with this. A suggested checklist is given in the Home Office booklet *Bombs: A Guide for Small Businesses*. Telephone the police immediately and decide whether to search or evacuate the premises.

In the event of evacuation, staff and clients must take their personal belongings with them to make any search procedures easier. Do not return to the premises until told to do so by the police or co-ordinator.

TIP BOX

The Home Office has produced two free booklets regarding bomb threats – *Bombs: A Guide for Small Businesses* and *Bombs: A Handbook for Managers and Security Officers*. Both are available from your local police CPO and contain much more information regarding bomb incidents. Further advice from the CPO should be obtained if you consider yourself to be in a high-risk category.

Telephone abuse

Unfortunately, the hair and beauty professions are prone to receiving unpleasant, obscene or upsetting phone calls. If you are on the receiving end of one of these calls, remember that the caller is deliberately trying to shock or upset you, so the first rule is not to react in any way whatsoever.

TIP BOX

An abusive telephone caller is trying to get a response from you. If you react angrily or emotionally to the call, you will encourage them to keep calling. Ignore them and they will usually stop calling.

Do not talk or argue with the caller or show anger, and definitely do not blow a whistle down the phone. Such actions will only encourage or provoke further calls. Be firm, stay calm, and do not give the caller the satisfaction of acting or sounding worried.

Once you have realised the call is malicious, do not say anything, but place the receiver down next to the phone and ignore it, walking away to get on with something else. Go back later and replace it. Do not listen to see if the caller is still on the line.

When the phone rings again, pick it up and do not say anything. A genuine caller will speak first. A malicious caller will ring off or make themselves known. If the caller is malicious, again do not react but place the receiver down next to the phone and walk away as before. Continue to behave in this manner with all malicious calls. If the caller is not getting any 'fun' from you, they will stop calling.

If these calls are a real, organised nuisance as opposed to an occasional occurrence, bear in mind that the making of malicious calls is a prosecutable offence. BT have a helpline which you can dial for further information regarding the prevention of these calls. The BT Malicious Calls Advice Line is available on 0800 666700.

Staff sometimes need protection from persistent unwanted callers at work. Salon policy should not allow casual incoming telephone calls to staff at work. Unless it is an emergency situation, callers will be told automatically that they cannot speak directly to the requested staff member and asked to leave a contact number. Under no circumstances should staff names, addresses, telephone numbers or hours of work be divulged to anyone without the permission of the staff member involved.

Fellow staff members

UNPLEASANT STAFF RIVALRY

This can be difficult to avoid, especially in a competitive situation. The need to be better than others arises for many reasons, e.g. promotion prospects, job security, financial gain – especially when wages are commission linked – and even problems with personal self-esteem.

One example of unpleasant rivalry is staff not booking clients for other members of staff, e.g. dominating the workload. Staff have been known to send casual clients away, asking them to come back later even though someone else could see them immediately. By doing this the staff member gains the client and the monetary commission. However, the salon and client do not always benefit. The client is inconvenienced and may not wait, but go elsewhere for their treatment. They may also not get the best person to do their type of hair or the treatment they want, or receive a rushed substandard treatment. This situation can arise even when a salon has a receptionist, if they have strong likes and dislikes among fellow staff members.

This is just one example of unpleasant staff rivalry; it can take many forms. It is best avoided by strong leadership and vigilance from the management or owners – simply do not allow this type of behaviour to take place. For example, client domination can be avoided by ensuring that more than one member of staff knows each client and their needs, so that they are interchangeable at busy times or during staff illness or holidays.

TIP BOX

Unpleasant rivalry will be less likely to arise if the staff feel that they are working as part of a team.

A sense of pride in the salon must be instilled in the staff, so that all work to the benefit of the whole instead of putting their individual, immediate needs first. Of course, this means that individual needs should be monitored and suitably met by the management so that problems do not arise. Regular individual and group staff meetings are important here. All staff management should be suitably trained in interpersonal skills so that they can spot and avoid petty jealousies and resentments, both real and imagined. Salon loyalty can be generated by group activities, both related to work (e.g. training events) and unrelated to work (e.g. sponsored charity events and staff outings).

STEALING FROM WORKMATES

All the points mentioned above in the section on staff rivalry will help prevent this situation arising, but it is still prudent not to put temptation in people's way. Staff need to be told not to bring valuables and large amounts of cash to work, and each staff member should be supplied with a secure locker at work in which they can safely store and lock their belongings.

TIP BOX

Never leave valuables in a staffroom unattended or clearly visible. The temptation to take them could prove too much to a workmate or outsider.

DRUG AND ALCOHOL ABUSE

This can be difficult to spot among staff and can cause problems, largely due to the erratic behaviour of the staff concerned. Drug and alcohol abuse cause changes in personality, for example a person who previously has been thoroughly honest may begin to steal from the salon or fellow staff members. They may begin to be late or absent from work. They may lose concentration at times, making mistakes in their work and being 'dreamy' and unconcerned about time schedules. Alternatively, if the problem progresses, they may become irritable, defensive and paranoid, thinking that people are watching and criticising them all the time. This in turn can escalate into verbal or physical violence. All this can happen over a long period of time, with workmates or the person in charge not being able to pinpoint the problem.

The more obvious signs of drug abuse, such as wraps, paper tubes, ends of hand-rolled cigarettes or syringes in toilets, are not usually apparent in small businesses where only a few staff members share the same toilet facilities – such evidence would be easily traceable to the offender. Less obvious signs are the users keeping their feet and arms covered to hide needle marks, or drug pushers waiting around outside the premises, as well as the personality changes already mentioned.

A drug-use situation can be very disturbing, and the only thing which can be done is to talk and keep talking regularly and frequently to the staff member concerned, giving support where possible. If the salon holds regular individual staff meetings, it will be possible to speak to the person involved without it seeming unusual to the rest of the staff.

If an employee is certain that a problem exists, with either themselves or a workmate, they should tell their superiors – the sooner the problem is tackled, the more chance there is of a positive outcome.

If help is requested, advise the person to seek help from their doctor. Encourage attendance at one of the Anonymous Twelve Step Groups, such as Alcoholics or Narcotics Anonymous. Their telephone numbers can be found in the telephone directory.

However, if help is refused and talking is met with denial when there obviously is a problem, then the welfare of the customers, other staff and the salon as a whole must take priority. Ultimately, the only person who can help the drug or alcohol abuser is themselves. They cannot be forced to obtain help.

TIP BOX

Have a clear policy on alcohol and drug use and make sure that employees know exactly what will happen to them if they ignore this.

In order to prevent problems with drugs and alcohol at work as far as possible, the owners or management should have a policy statement regarding drugs and alcohol written into the employee's work contract. Such a policy could stipulate, for example, that there should be no drinking at lunchtimes and no smoking on the premises. It may even reserve the right to carry out on-the-spot drug screening and testing.

SEXUAL HARASSMENT AND BULLYING

This is a huge area which receives a lot of media coverage. Incidents are often a means of one person achieving power or control over another, taking advantage of a person's vulnerability to get what they want.

Bullying or harassment can make a person behave and respond in a helpless, uncharacteristic manner, or even cause them to leave the workplace. Driving a person to resign because they find their work situation unbearable is sometimes known as constructive dismissal. It is a well-recognised problem in the workplace (see page 17).

This section will focus on sexual harassment because of its complexity, but the methods employed to deal with this can be adapted to deal with harassment or bullying of any sort, from both workmates and clients.

Prevention

Prevention is always better than cure, and the main way to prevent harassment or misunderstanding is to first take a good look at yourself. How do you present yourself to others? What do they perceive you to be?

Most people have never had cause or opportunity to really explore themselves as a person, sitting down and thinking about how they actually present themselves to others as opposed to how they want to be seen. Margaret Thatcher is a prime example of a person who did just this. She set her goal (being prime minister); looked at how she could better present herself to achieve that goal (by modulating her voice, wearing businesslike but feminine clothing, and altering her hair and make-up); and then did these things so that people accepted her as a powerful person who meant business. Would she have been taken seriously as a person competent to run a country had she been dressed in short skirts and revealing blouses, with false eyelashes, lashings of eyeliner and mascara and long, scarlet-painted artificial fingernails? We might rebel against such stereotypes, but they are a fact and cannot be ignored. Even in the law courts, a woman rape victim walking home alone down a back alley at two o'clock in the morning wearing a micro skirt, skimpy top and stilettos is often deemed to have contributed to her rape by her appearance.

This stereotyping is not confined to women. A man who dresses in a feminine way and uses a feminine tone of voice and mannerisms may be labelled as 'gay' and unfortunately be harassed, bullied or even attacked because of this. Sometimes, simply being a male hairdresser is sufficient to cause problems of this type!

Define your boundaries

The best place to explore yourself in relation to these issues is in an assertiveness training class. Here you can define your boundaries, i.e. identify how you want to be seen and treated both in work and out of work (for the two can often be different), and learn how to achieve this.

Bearing in mind how certain actions can be misinterpreted by others, it is often best to err on the side of caution at work, adopting a non-sexual, non-threatening, but professional attitude both in behaviour and dress.

Combining work and romance is seldom a good idea. Dating a workmate can often make it harder to concentrate on work; more difficult to maintain a balanced view of or end the relationship; and if the relationship does end unpleasantly, it can make the working situation difficult. Gossip about your relationship or behaviour could undermine any position of authority at work, or your promotion prospects, and the fact that you have had a romantic liaison with one workmate may signal your availability to others.

Also in this context, it is important to be consistent at work, not behaving one way with one person and another way with another, as this could be perceived as favouritism and cause jealousy and other similar problems.

Act immediately

Once you have decided how you wish to be treated by others (set your boundaries), adhere to these strictly in a no-nonsense, non-sexual way, not allowing grey areas. For example, if someone pats your bottom when passing, rebuff the action immediately with a strong, firm and loud 'stop that!' This open and often unexpected response is often sufficient to stop the person from doing it again. You have demonstrated how much you are prepared to accept; you have 'set your boundaries'.

This is often the time when low self-esteem causes the recipient to pause and wonder, 'Did they? Didn't they? I must have imagined it. It must have been my fault for getting in their way.' *Don't do this.* It happened. Follow your instincts and respond immediately. If you are wrong, a quick apology will put things right, and the person and any witnesses will know never to do that to you in future.

Confrontation

If the harassment is more subtle, then an organised 'confrontation' is the best approach. Ask the person involved for some time to talk to them privately about an important issue. Practise what you are going to say, in confidence, with someone senior or a sensible supportive friend at work. This practice is invaluable for helping you to formulate the most tactful but clear and effective way of phrasing your words. Take this person along to the meeting as an impartial and non-threatening witness.

The object of this meeting is to clear the air and set acceptable boundaries for a future pleasant working situation. Therefore do not start by verbally attacking or accusing the person. Keep calm and follow these guidelines:

- **Make the person think about why they acted in this way**. They need to address this issue if they are to see your side of the problem and change their behaviour. For example, say 'Do you realise the effect your patting me on the bottom every time you walk past has on me?'
- **State your feelings.** People cannot argue with how you feel. For example, say 'It makes me feel really humiliated in front of the customers and other staff members.'
- **Ask for the change you want.** The person cannot do what you want unless you ask for it directly. For example, say 'I want you to stop doing it.'
- Follow this with the **consequence** of the person complying with your request and try to keep this positive. For example, say 'I will feel much happier and more relaxed at work if you do stop.'
- **End on a positive note.** This shows that there are no ill feelings. For example, say 'I'm glad to have had this chance to talk to you.'

Sometimes a final positive comment to show that you value the other person as a workmate helps to keep the incident in perspective. A negative consequence such as 'I will have to look for a job elsewhere' should not be said lightly and should possibly be held back for a future confrontation if the first one fails. Only say as much as you are

prepared to act upon, as failure will undermine your confidence and could escalate the situation.

If the harassment continues after these measures and is unacceptable, then you must keep notes of incidents which occur, their dates, times and places, and names of witnesses to them. Gather concrete information such as letters, notes or tape recordings, while still making attempts to resolve the issue through the proper channels. Then take this information to your supervisors asking for the situation to be remedied. Do not part with any of this information; make copies where necessary. If this final attempt fails, take the matter outside the workplace to seek further advice. Your local Citizens Advice Bureau can be helpful here.

CONSTRUCTIVE DISMISSAL

Constructive dismissal is the term used when a person finds their conditions of work unbearable, and their legitimate and substantiated complaints are not being dealt with seriously by the people in authority – so much so that the only option they feel they have left is to resign. In such cases the employee may apply for their case to be heard by an Industrial Tribunal. The employee may be able to claim compensation, although they will still have lost their job and they may find it difficult to get further employment. Regardless of the outcome of a court case, they can find their future job prospects severely limited by the prejudice of other employers who may label them as troublemakers. It is far better to be able to resolve the problem at work through the proper channels.

> **TIP BOX**
>
> If you find interpersonal relationships difficult, an assertiveness training course can often help. Choose one where role-playing situations are held, as there is a huge difference between reading about how to handle a situation and actually dealing with it in practice. If a course is not available, books such as Anne Dickson's *A Woman in Your Own Right: Assertiveness and You* can provide valuable information and assistance. (Men can benefit from reading this too.)

PART TWO

Accident prevention and safety in the salon

Many of the working situations and the treatments carried out in a hairdressing or beauty therapy salon are inherently dangerous, both to the practitioner and the client. Recently trained hairdressers or therapists, leaving the fully supervised environment of the training college, are suddenly very much on their own, even in the largest of establishments.

Mistakes can easily happen, and can have many causes. They can be a result of misunderstandings, such as not realising that a new product or piece of equipment is not used in quite the same way as the old one. Or they can be due to a simple oversight, for example forgetting to check the temperature of rinsing water or a spatula of wax.

Practising hairdressers and therapists have often discovered such pitfalls the hard way, injuring themselves, or upsetting or losing a few clients as they gained in experience and expertise.

A hairdresser or therapist who is aware of what could happen in the workplace or during and after a treatment (and why) is better able to prevent many of these mishaps occurring. This part of the book aims to supply the therapist with this information. It guides the therapist and hairdresser through safe working practices and the various treatments as they should be carried out on a daily basis, establishing the safest procedures and pointing out potential hazards.

Listed alphabetically on the following pages are various work situations, items of equipment and specific treatments, along with the possible dangers inherent in each and how best to avoid these dangers.

For ease of use, this part has been divided into three sections covering situations:

1. in **general**, i.e. common to all hair, health and beauty therapy salons and clinics (pages 21–49). This section includes simple but thorough coverage of current rules and regulations affecting these industries
2. specific to **beauty, nail and health** salons and clinics (pages 50–77)
3. specific to **hairdressing** salons (pages 78–94).

Although this text provides useful guidelines, nothing can take the place of experience. Hairdressers and therapists must concentrate on their working situation and their work to the maximum of their ability at all times, and be constantly on the alert for anything unusual.

They must continually remind themselves that each client is an individual and is not pre-programmed to react to a treatment in the same way as anyone else, or even as they reacted to the same treatment the last time they had it! If hairdressers and therapists are conscientious in this way, the chances of mishaps and accidents occurring at work will be substantially reduced.

Back care and lifting

• • • • • • • • DANGERS • • • • • • • •

Backache, 'slipped' disk, sciatica, muscle and ligament strain, muscular spasms.

• • • • • • • PRECAUTIONS • • • • • • • •

Many injuries are caused by incorrect lifting or working postures. In all activities the spine must be kept as straight as possible. It may seem difficult at first to change the way you usually do things. However, it is important to adopt the correct posture because if the back is damaged it can cause persistent trouble or permanent injury.

1. Do not do jobs which your physical strength is not capable of, e.g. too much massaging, or unloading boxes of heavy stock from a vehicle. If something is too heavy, leave it until you can get help. The recommended maximum weights for a fit person to lift are 25 kilos for a woman and 50 kilos for a man.

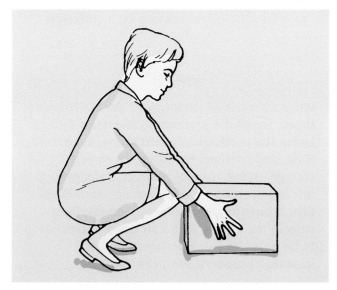

The correct lifting posture

2. If the load is manageable but heavy, drag it with one arm and the body sideways so that the back is kept straight.
3. Bend your knees, not your back, when lifting an object or picking something up off the floor.
4. Hold heavy objects close to your body. Holding things at arm's length puts a tremendous strain on the back.
5. Move around a massage bed, sunbed, client, etc. rather than leaning over to work, change covers or clean.
6. Kneel down to activities at ground level, e.g. body wrap, cutting children's hair, etc. Avoid bending over.
7. When sitting, choose a chair which has no lower back to it. Push your bottom right back into the chair so that your weight is resting on the thighs. Adjust the height of the chair so that your feet are flat on the floor. Do not cross your legs as this twists and places a strain on the pelvis and spine. Leg crossing can also place pressure on the circulation at the back of the knees and be a contributory factor in the development of varicose veins.

TIP BOX

The 'health and safety' recommended chair of use is the five-castor movable chair with adjustable height and backrest, sometimes known as the 'super secretarial chair'.

8. When sitting down or standing up, do not stick your bottom out, jut your head forward or throw it back. Maintain the alignment of the spine, neck and head, bending only at the hips, knees and ankles.
9. The standing position can also cause problems. This is especially the case with hairdressers and any therapists who have a tendency to work

with their upper body, arms and head inclined forwards. Ideally, the ears, shoulders, hips and ankles should be in a straight line at right angles to the floor.

10 Hairdressers and therapists spend a lot of time working with their arms forward and this unnatural posture will ultimately lead to problems with their neck and shoulder muscles. This can be avoided by receiving a regular, thorough back, neck and shoulder massage.

A multi-posture stool

Chemicals

• • • • • • • • DANGERS • • • • • • • •

Fires, poisoning, spillage, leakage, corrosion, degradation, allergy, inhalation, swallowing, chemical burns, explosion, exposure to light.

• • • • • • • PRECAUTIONS • • • • • • • •

1 Most products used in hairdressing, beauty and therapy workplaces are potentially hazardous and need to be handled with care. They may be

Hazard symbols

inflammable, corrosive, toxic, combustible, and/or give off poisonous or inflammable fumes. Examples of such chemicals are formaldehyde solutions (which are used in vapour sterilising cabinets), hydrogen peroxide (which is used in bleaching, perming and tinting), bleaching agents, hair colours, setting lotions, shampoos, cans of hairspray and mousses, skin-peeling preparations, essential oils, nail polish, nail repair and extension materials, acetone, sterilising solutions (e.g. glutaraldehydes), and cleansing materials such as bleach and disinfectants.

2 Before handling and storing any hazardous materials, chemicals and liquids, always refer to the manufacturer's data sheets as required by the Control of Substances Hazardous to Health (COSHH) Regulations 1994 (see page 24). These data sheets give information about the correct storage and disposal of the product, any potential danger which may be incurred by

using or storing the product, and the correct first-aid procedure to be followed if an accident happens involving the product, e.g. inhalation, swallowing, eye or skin contact.

3   Store hazardous, corrosive, volatile and inflammable chemicals, including liquids containing alcohol, e.g. lacquer, spirit setting lotions, methylated spirits (70% alcohol), surgical spirit, artificial nail liquids, nail varnish and removers (solvents), in metal or strong glass containers. Where this is not possible (many such products are bought already packaged in plastic containers), they should be stored standing in drip trays which are big enough to hold the contents if they should leak out of the container. In this way a potentially hazardous leakage will be contained.

4   Where glass is used to store chemicals, make sure that it is non-actinic where appropriate, i.e. will not allow the contents to be affected by light. All glass bottles should be stored below eye level to avoid potential accidents.

TIP BOX

Baking trays and containers make cheap and ideal drip trays.

5   Other chemicals which are not corrosive or inflammable should be kept, where possible, in plastic or polythene containers, thus reducing the dangers of breakage.

TIP BOX

Plastic is more susceptible to corrosion and damage during transit than metal or strong glass. Check new deliveries carefully.

6   All stores of hazardous volatile or inflammable chemicals, together with hydrogen peroxide, ammonia and permanent waving solutions, must be kept in a cool place in a securely locked fireproof cabinet, away from direct sunlight and the main workplace. Large

containers should be kept on the lowest shelves to reduce the risk of accidents in handling. *Do not* store combustible materials with inflammable materials. *Do not* store combustible or inflammable materials near a source of heat, fuel or ignition, e.g. boilers, gas, electricity or flames.

TIP BOX

A fireproof cabinet will withstand a fire for 30 minutes. If there is a fire, the fire brigade must be told immediately where this cabinet is and how long the fire has been burning.

7   Clearly label all bottles and jars to indicate their contents and their actual strength where applicable. Labels must be used which are resistant to the contents of the container. When pouring or handling liquids, always ensure that the label is facing you. In this way, contact between the label and the contents of the container is avoided, thus minimising any damage to the label.

8   Aerosols must be stored in a cool place and, when empty, disposed of in accordance with the manufacturer's instructions. Hairdressers need to take care that they do not use sharp objects near or on aerosol cans, e.g. to prise off the lids, as there is a real risk of puncturing the cans. If this were to happen near a fire or lighted cigarette, a fatal fire could result. Aerosols must never be disposed of in a fire as they will explode.

TIP BOX

Do not use aerosol cans or other inflammable products in window displays, where the heat from the sun may cause ignition.

9   All storage areas must be kept cool as bacterial growth and chemical degradation (breakdown) tends to develop faster in the warm conditions of the workplace.

10 A prominent sign must be displayed on the front of all chemical storage areas, e.g. **'Danger. Poisonous and inflammable chemicals. Keep away from children. No smoking allowed.'**

11 Any spillage must be cleaned up immediately using whatever is recommended in the relevant substance data sheets. For example, for permanent waving solutions this may be plain water initially, followed by neutral cleansing materials so that unwanted and possibly dangerous chemical reactions do not occur. In the case of essential oils, sand would be used to soak up the spillage. In all cases, the floor must be dried off thoroughly afterwards to avoid people slipping.

Control of Substances Hazardous to Health (COSHH) Regulations 1994

• • • • • • • • DANGERS • • • • • • • •

Injury to health by contact with, breathing in, swallowing, injecting or otherwise introducing into the body any substance which may cause harm; prosecution through not keeping the relevant documentation available for inspection.

• • • • • • • PRECAUTIONS • • • • • • •

1 Employers must, by law, identify, list and assess in writing any substances in the workplace, e.g. bleach, essential oils, acetone-based nail varnish remover, artificial nail products and glues, glutaraldehyde solutions, shampoos and conditioners, regardless of whether they may be hazardous to health or not. These substances must be given a hazard rating, even if it is 0 (see risk assessment, page 43). Employers must also identify, list and assess in writing which employees are at risk, not forgetting occasional workers, e.g. cleaners. These assessments must be reviewed regularly (not more than five years or every time a change occurs).

2 Read the COSHH data sheets for all products used in the salon or clinic. Inform and train your staff regarding what they say, and abide by their recommendations for use, storage and first aid. Keep copies for staff reference.

Ellisons

AEROSOLS
Health hazard: flammable.

Use/handling: Use only in a well-ventilated area. Do not smoke whilst in use. Keep away from eyes. Avoid excessive inhalation of spray. Do not spray onto naked flame or hot surfaces. Do not warm cans or tamper with the valve/actuator to ease removal of contents.

Storage: Keep in a cool dry place. Protect from sunlight. Avoid window displays which are exposed to sun. Do not expose to excessive temperatures.

Disposal: Do not pierce or burn aerosol container. Contents are under pressure and they can cause an explosion in a fire.

Action: In case of fire, evacuate areas known to contain aerosols and inform fire service of their existence.

Beauty products which can be packed in aerosol form are:

> Ambersil Glass Cleaner
> Ambersil Surface Cleaner
> Nail Dry Sprays
> Hairspray

01.05.94

A sample COSHH data sheet

TIP BOX

Manufacturers have to supply COSHH data sheets for all their products. Make sure that you obtain them for *every* product you use.

3 If a choice of products is available, use one which causes the least hazard to health in any given situation.

4 Where a hazard still exists, personal protective equipment (PPE – see page 39) must be provided free of charge by the employer and the employee taught how to use it correctly. Measures must also be taken to limit exposure to the product, e.g. by installing proper ventilation equipment.

TIP BOX

A leaflet called *Five Steps for Completing COSHH Assessments* is available free from your local Health and Safety Executive (HSE) office. Also available are *COSHH: A Brief Guide for Employers* (IND(G) 136L(Rev)), and *COSHH Assessments: A Step By Step Guide* (ISBN 0 11 886379 7). All HSE publications are available from HSE Books (address on page 122).

Cosmetic products

Cosmetic products include make-up, nail varnish and varnish remover, cleansers, toners, moisturisers, masks, coloured and clear setting lotions, semi-permanent colours, gels, crazy colours, conditioners, lacquers, shampoos and hair sprays. Also included in this group are any other products with which the employer, employee or client is likely to come into contact, e.g. antiseptics, disinfectants, bleaches and surgical spirit.

TIP BOX

COSHH Regulations apply to all these products. Follow precaution 2 in the section on chemicals (page 22).

• • • • • • • • DANGERS • • • • • • • •

Allergic reactions, skin sensitivity, burns, inhalation, swallowing of any products, contact dermatitis.

• • • • • • • • PRECAUTIONS • • • • • • • •

1 Question each client carefully for any previous allergic reactions, e.g. food, cosmetics or washing powders, as this could indicate sensitivity to chemical products. Asthma or hay fever, in particular, indicate a person who may be prone to allergies.
2 Where there is any doubt regarding the sensitivity of a client to a particular product (e.g. when using a product on a client for the first time), it is advisable to carry out a skin test 48 hours prior to treatment (see page 44, skin testing). Be aware that allergic reactions may be triggered by the most bland of products, or products which have produced no reaction in the same person before.

TIP BOX

Sometimes manufacturers change the formulation of their products without adequate notification, and this could result in an allergic reaction in a client where there was previously none. Be aware of this when buying new stock.

3 During each new treatment on a client, keep careful watch for any signs of skin sensitivity or allergy, e.g. extreme redness or stinging. Discontinue the treatment and apply first aid immediately if this happens.

TIP BOX

Use of HRT, the contraceptive pill, or medication, plus the stage of the menstrual cycle, can all lead to sensitivities and allergy reactions occurring.

4 Keep extensive client records with dates of treatments, products used and reaction, if any (see page 40).

TIP BOX

Products which the client uses at home can affect and react with professional treatment products, e.g. all-in-one shampoos and conditioners, and chlorine from swimming baths.

5 Never use solutions which are too strong. Always take care to follow the recommended dilutions for antiseptics and disinfectants.
6 Keep all products well away from the eyes.
7 Keep all products well out of reach of any waiting children.

8 Where it is the hairdresser or beautician who shows sensitivity to cosmetic products, special care must be taken to use barrier creams and protective equipment whenever necessary. Sensitivities and reactions must be reported to the employer and checked by an occupational health doctor as soon as possible. Extreme and untreated cases could result in the hairdresser or beauty therapist having to discontinue the occupation.

Electrical equipment

• • • • • • • • • DANGERS • • • • • • • • •

Electric shocks, electrical burns, falls due to trailing wires, fires due to electrical faults, death due to electrocution. Around 1,000 electric shock accidents at work are reported to the HSE each year.

• • • • • • • • PRECAUTIONS • • • • • • • •

1 All electrical appliances must be correctly fused and 'earthed' in accordance with the British Standards Institution's recommended practice. Even the hot and cold water pipes must be connected together and earthed. It is also recommended that a residual current device (earth leakage trip) rated at 30 mA should be fitted in the circuits to which any movable or hand tools are connected, e.g. hand dryers, electric clippers, G5 machines and hand-held massagers, electrolysis machines, etc.

TIP BOX

As from January 1996, all new electrical appliances have to be stamped with the CE mark to show that they have reached a set standard of electrical safety.

2 Every six months, all frequently used electrical equipment, e.g. hand-held hair dryers or manicure drills, needs to be inspected and tested by a competent person with sufficient training in basic electrical knowledge. This person does not need to be a qualified electrician, but can be the employer or an employee. If they are able to make any necessary repairs, e.g. change a plug, fuse or frayed cable, they should do so. If not, then a qualified electrician should be used. Checks should be made on:

- connecting wires to ensure that they are not frayed or cut, or the flex melted
- wire insertions into apparatus and plugs to ensure that they are not becoming loose
- plugs to make sure that they are correctly fused and wired and that the wires are in good condition and not working loose. The wire inside the cable can begin to break at the insertion into the plug or appliance, leading to a faulty connection
- adaptors to see that they are not overloaded
- on/off switches to make sure that they are functioning safely and properly
- the general condition of all the electrical equipment. Is the outer cover sound and all screws tight? Is the appliance wet, damp or dusty? Are there any overheating (burn) marks?

TIP BOX

Do not forget to include any extension leads, sockets and plugs in your checks.

3 Appliances which are not used as frequently or moved around as much should be inspected and tested every 12 months.

4 To make sure that all the electrical items are checked, a list (maintenance log) containing the description, make and serial number of all the electrical equipment in the workplace should be made and each item labelled with its correct number. New items should be added to this list and discarded ones removed. Having a list means that items which are often overlooked, such as vacuum cleaners, coffee makers, washers, dryers, electric tills and adding machines, spotlights, immersion heaters, time switches and sterilisers, will all be given a regular safety check. Keep a record on this list of the date when the equipment was last checked and the person who checked it. Also include details of any defects found and repairs made.

5 As so many of the electrical appliances used in hair and beauty salons are hand-held and frequently used, e.g. hair dryers and G5 machines, a quick visual check of these electrical appliances, plugs and connecting wiring should be made before every use. If an appliance is found to be faulty, clearly label it as 'out of use' and put it away where other people are not likely to find and use it until it is mended.

> ## TIP BOX
>
> **Damaged or chipped plugs must never be used. They could lead to electric shock, especially if touched with wet hands.**

6 Complex equipment and equipment which is not moved around much, e.g. computers, electrolysis machines and accelerators, should be checked and tested annually by the competent person as above, and/or by the service engineers of the company of manufacture every 1–5 years. When equipment is bought, contracts for regular servicing can often be taken out with the company for a small additional charge. Do remember that any attempted repair or adjustment of this type of equipment by anyone other than the manufacturer's own service engineers will negate any warranty or guarantee and absolve the manufacturer from all responsibility for repairing the machine under the terms of the sales contract.

7 Make sure that wires are not left trailing across floors or any spaces. Equipment must be plugged into a socket in the same area where it is used. If a length of flex is needed when using the equipment, e.g. for hand massagers or blow-drying equipment, then coiled wires (like telephone receiver wires) are available which will stretch and retract very easily, thus avoiding trailing wires.

8 Check that any appliance involving a thermostat, e.g. a wax heater or fixed position dryer, is functioning at the correct temperature each time it is used, just in case the thermostat has broken.

9 Care must always be taken to keep water away from electrical equipment or sockets. You must not be able to reach a plug socket or electrical appliance at the same time as a source of water. In hairdressing salons, it is not always easy to keep to this rule. Special covered sockets will increase safety, but great care must be taken where water and electricity are close together. Certain appliances, e.g. electric foot baths, steamers, steam baths and saunas, use water in them. Extra care must be taken with the servicing of these appliances and they should be checked at least every six months.

> ## TIP BOX
>
> **It is extremely dangerous to use electric appliances with wet hands. Extra care must be taken around wet hair; for safety, hold the hair dryer in one hand and the blow-dry brush in the other.**

10 Plug sockets must not be overloaded because this may cause overheating and subsequent fires. The maximum wattage going through a standard 13 amp socket must not exceed 3,120 watts. Make sure that any adaptors used in the salon are not overloaded by checking the wattage of the equipment plugged into them. A sunbed with a top and bottom unit may use 20×100 watts for the bulbs, plus the cooling fans and, perhaps, an additional fan by the side of the bed. If these are all run off one socket with the use of an adaptor, this could easily result in overheating and a possible fire. If it is necessary to run a few high wattage items off one socket (up to the maximum value), then special, fused electrical adaptors can be bought for this purpose. A standard adaptor is not sufficient. Ideally, separate sockets should be used.

> ## TIP BOX
>
> **An overheated plug emits a powerful 'fishy' odour as it overheats. If this smell occurs, check around the plug points immediately.**

11 Mobile pieces of equipment, e.g. hand-held dryers, often have long straight flexes. When putting these away, take care not to fold the cable into a hairpin bend as this could produce a weak spot which might break and cause a short circuit.

12 Make sure that the salon or clinic possesses fire extinguishers capable of dealing with electrical fires. They must be kept within easy reach and all employees should know how to use them (see fire safety, page 29).

13 Do not allow clients to touch any electrical equipment.

14 Make sure that all electrical appliances are unplugged or otherwise disconnected before leaving the workplace. An easy way to do this is to install on/off switches with lit or red indicators so that it can be seen at a glance if the power is still on. Pressing the switch off at the end of work is easier than unplugging the appliance and causes less wear and tear on the cable/plug junction. Note: if the plug is removed, the switch should be off before the plug is pulled out.

TIP BOX

As a general rule in England, light and plug switches are off when up and on when down – but not if they are capable of being activated from more than one place, e.g. the top and bottom of a staircase.

15 Old-style electric fan heaters with coiled wire elements inside should be avoided where there is any danger of liquids being spilled on to them. More modern fan heaters contain ceramic elements which are much safer.

16 Plug fuses prevent surges of electric current from going to the appliance and electrocuting

the operator. The fuse melts if such a power surge occurs, and thus disconnects the appliance from the mains electricity. Standard plug fuses are available in 3, 5 and 13 amp ratings. When fitting a fuse into a plug, make sure that it has the correct rating for the appliance concerned. If it is too high, it will not melt with a power surge and electrocution could occur. As a rough guideline, 2.5–3 amps of fuse should be used for every 500 watts of appliance, e.g. a 1,000 watt hair dryer would need a 5 amp fuse fitted into the attached plug.

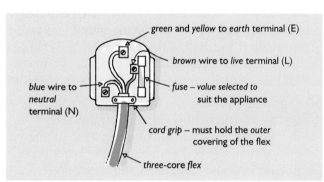

green and yellow to earth terminal (E)

brown wire to live terminal (L)

blue wire to neutral terminal (N)

fuse – value selected to suit the appliance

cord grip – must hold the outer covering of the flex

three-core flex

John V. Simmons

Wiring a plug

TIP BOX

The main fuse box contains fuses with very high ratings to service different areas of the premises. If possible, label each fuse with the area it serves, e.g. upstairs lights, upstairs sockets, so that the relevant areas can be rapidly isolated or the fuse repaired when necessary.

17 The maximum safe load on a standard ring main is 30 amps (9,000 watts). Beyond these values, special thick cable capable of carrying more current from the mains to the appliance is installed and the appliance is connected directly into its own high-rating fuse box, e.g. 40 amps for an electric shower, 60 amps for a large sunbed or electric cooker.

TIP BOX

Make sure that all staff know where the main fuse box and mains switch are so that the power can be turned off quickly in an emergency.

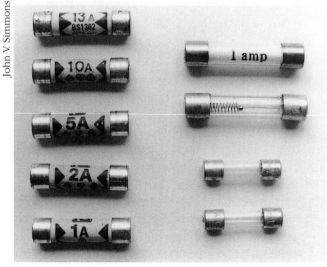

John V. Simmons

Fuses

Eye strain

• • • • • • • • DANGERS • • • • • • • •

Blurred vision, inability to focus on objects at different distances quickly or at all, deterioration of eyesight.

• • • • • • • PRECAUTIONS • • • • • • •

1 Long periods of concentrated close work, e.g. manicure and artificial nail extension work, electrolysis, tweezer epilation, tattooing and computer screen work (VDU), should be avoided. At the very least, regular breaks should be taken or the workload planned so that there are changes in activities. A break of ten minutes in every hour where the eyes are being used to focus on other things at different distances is recommended.

2 Blink often, once or twice every ten seconds, and pause to look up briefly approximately every five minutes to focus on something further away.

3 Make sure that good lighting is available (and used) at all work stations.

TIP BOX

This is a useful exercise to revive tired eyes. Twice a day, or whenever the eyes feel tired, close your eyes and cover them with cupped palms. Relax and continue the exercise for ten minutes.

4 Anyone having problems with their eyesight should have their eyes checked by an optician. If the problems are work related, the employer may have to pay for special glasses for work. As well as consulting an optician, an alternative approach to eye care, the **Bates method** of eye exercises, is worth investigating.

Fire safety

See also first aid, page 99.

• • • • • • • • DANGERS • • • • • • • •

Hairdressing or beauty salons are particularly at risk from fire because of the amounts of electrical equipment they contain. This, together with the inflammable chemicals which are in daily use (e.g. lacquer sprays, nail varnish remover, essential oils), and the number of people who pass through, means that the salon is potentially a very dangerous place indeed.

• • • • • • • PRECAUTIONS • • • • • • •

1 The Fire Precautions Act 1971 states that there must be a reasonable means of escape from a shop premises in the event of fire and that this escape must be no more than 18 metres from any given point in the shop. The escape door must be kept unlocked whenever anyone is on the premises. The door and the pathway to it must be clearly labelled.

TIP BOX

If there are fire doors on the way to the exit, make sure you shut them as you leave in order to contain the fire. Windows too should be closed to deprive the fire of oxygen and help contain it. However, the main priority in case of fire is to get out of the building. Fire doors must always be kept closed but not locked if anyone is on the premises, and they must be free from obstruction, e.g. chairs, so that people can leave easily.

2 The Act also states that suitable fire-fighting apparatus must be readily available. The most suitable single piece of equipment for a hairdressing or therapy premises is a dry-powder extinguisher, colour-coded blue, which is capable of dealing with all types of fires, e.g. flammable liquid, electrical, upholstery, etc. One extinguisher should be provided for every 200 square metres of floor space.

TIP BOX

Fire extinguishers containing water must *never* be used on an electrical or flammable liquid fire.

TIP BOX

Until recently, fire extinguishers came in different colours depending on their contents, e.g. dry-powder fire extinguishers were blue. As from January 1997, *all* fire extinguishers will be red, but they will have different-coloured markings on them to indicate their contents, e.g. blue markings indicate dry powder. This is to comply with the British Standards Regulation EN3, brought out to meet current European Regulations. The old coloured fire extinguishers can still be used as long as they are working properly.

A range of fire extinguishers

3 Extinguishers must be placed on an exit route so that if a person goes to get an extinguisher and then finds the fire is too much to handle, they are on their way out of the premises and not backed into a corner and unable to escape. **Make sure that all staff know how to use the extinguishers.**

TIP BOX

It is useful to keep an extra, small dry-powder extinguisher, such as the type sold for use in cars, next to any area where a problem is likely to occur, e.g. the main fuse box.

4 When buying the main extinguishers, do not buy from doorstep salesmen, but telephone a reputable company listed in the *Yellow Pages*. In this way, reliable equipment and aftercare service at a reasonable price are ensured. By law, an arrangement must be made to have the equipment inspected every 12 months to check that it is in correct working order. Remember to have fire extinguishers replaced or refilled immediately after use. If there is a fire and the extinguishers are found not to have been maintained correctly, or the guidelines not followed, your insurance company may refuse to meet your claim.

5 The use of inflammable products in hairdressing and beauty therapy workplaces, e.g. hair lacquers, nail varnish removers and essential oils, means that open fires, e.g. gas or electric bar fires, and smoking should be avoided.

6 A fire blanket is a useful additional piece of equipment to have in the salon – it can be used to smother flames if a person catches fire.

A fire blanket

TIP BOX

Smoke alarms can be cheaply and easily obtained and it is sensible to install one in every room.

7 Make sure that notices are displayed to inform people what to do in the event of fire, and that the fire exits are well marked. Fire exit doors should be kept free from obstruction and unlocked during working hours and when anyone is on the premises.

TIP BOX

Regular fire drills will ensure that staff know how to cope in the event of a fire.

8 If a small fire does occur, and it is successfully brought under control using existing equipment, it is still advisable to call the fire brigade. Many fires occur out of working hours after a small fire, which was thought to have been extinguished satisfactorily, has smouldered, hidden behind a wall, floorboard or ceiling, only to erupt into life many hours later. The fire brigade is trained to look for this sort of problem and their expertise should be taken advantage of – quite possibly preventing a tragedy by doing so.

9 A serious fire *has* to be reported to your local Environmental Health Officer, immediately by telephone and then using form F2508 (see RIDDOR, page 122) which is available from the HSE.

TIP BOX

Many companies supply videos and/or training packs about what to do in the event of fire in the workplace. An annual staff training session could be used to watch and work through one of these.

10 If the business has 20 or more employees, or is adjoining another business and the total number of employees for the combined businesses is 20 or more (e.g. a health club adjoining a hairdresser and a beauty salon), the premises needs to carry a current fire certificate (Fire Precautions Act 1971). Contact the Fire Prevention Officer at your local fire brigade station to obtain this.

Fire inspection

In order to comply with the 1971 Fire Precautions Act, the local authority (usually the Environmental Health section) must be notified of any new business or change of ownership of an existing business.

This notification sets in motion a series of visits from inspectors belonging to various local authority departments. If the business has over 20 employees, the Fire Prevention Officer will inspect the premises

TIP BOX

You can register your business on Form OSR1, available from your local council (Office, Shops and Railway Premises Act 1963).

and interview the owner or manager with regard to fire safety provisions. Thereafter, the Fire Prevention Officer will make a routine inspection every 4–5 years to check that the fire-fighting equipment and escape facilities are being maintained in full working order. The officer will check that staff know how to use the equipment and that circumstances have not changed, i.e. requiring updating or expansion of current facilities.

TIP BOX

This situation *may* at some future date be replaced by one of self-regulation even for workplaces with over 20 employees. An initial clearance will be given by the fire brigade, but it will then be the responsibility of the owner to maintain and update the provisions for fire prevention and safety. Check this with your Fire Prevention Officer.

The Fire Prevention Officer can always be contacted at the local fire station if it is felt that any advice is needed or to organise an inspection of your premises, no matter how small your establishment. Likewise, contact the officer if you feel that an additional check should be made for any reason, e.g. the installation of an extra sunbed or a new lighting system, or expansion of the premises. In many circumstances, it is best to contact the Fire Prevention Officer for advice before such changes are made.

TIP BOX

There is a possibility that all shop premises may be required to have fire alarms and emergency lighting at some future date (EC Places of Work Act – still under discussion). Bear this in mind when designing or changing your premises.

Gas appliances

• • • • • • • • • DANGERS • • • • • • • • •

Carbon monoxide poisoning, fire, suffocation, leakage, explosion.

• • • • • • • • PRECAUTIONS • • • • • • • •

I Use of gas is controlled by the Gas Safety Regulations 1994 (updated 1996). If gas is used in the workplace, a once yearly visit by a CORGI-registered gas engineer must be arranged to service all the gas appliances, e.g. gas boilers, water heaters, heaters and central heating systems, and to check the flues and pipework. This annual safety check is required by law. The Gas Board offers such service contracts. Do-it-yourself installation or repair work on gas appliances is illegal. By law you must not use any gas appliance which you know or suspect to be unsafe.

TIP BOX

The gas engineer must be CORGI registered. Ask to see a current CORGI registration certificate or telephone CORGI on 01256 372300 to confirm registration.

2 If any part of the premises is being sublet for domestic use, the person subletting (the landlord) is liable by law for the annual maintenance of gas pipework, flues and any gas appliances, e.g. gas boilers, water heaters and central heating systems, as above. Any appliances owned and brought in by the tenant at a later date are the responsibility of the tenant.

3 If part of the premises is being let or sublet for commercial use, e.g. a hairdresser renting a room to a beauty therapist, it must be made clear in the renting agreement who is responsible for the annual maintenance of gas pipework, flues and appliances. If it is the tenant, a written agreement placing the responsibility on the tenant must be signed jointly by the tenant and landlord. Any appliances owned by the tenant and brought in at a later date are the responsibility of the tenant.

4 A maintenance record for gas appliances must be kept, listing all the appliances, the date last serviced and/or checked, any defects, and repairs needed and carried out. This record, or a copy, must by law be given to the tenant and be available for an inspector to see at any time.

5 If an appliance is not functioning correctly, it must be disconnected by the engineer and prominently labelled as unsuitable for use until it is repaired.

TIP BOX

Before installing any gas appliances, contact the Gas Board's Commercial Department to arrange an advisory inspection. They will give advice on safety measures, ventilation, air bricks, size, type and position of boilers and fires, etc.

6 Any installation of gas appliances must be carried out by suitably qualified (CORGI registered) gas engineers to ensure that the regulations regarding siting, pipework, installation and adequate ventilation are followed.

TIP BOX

Make sure that all employees know where the mains gas stopcock is so that the gas supply can be turned off completely in an emergency. The general rule with stopcocks is that you turn the tap anticlockwise for on and clockwise for off. When turning the supply on, turn the tap fully until it stops, then turn it back half a turn to stop it from 'locking'. It is sensible to label the tap and keep instructions next to it.

7 A distinctive smell is added to gas so that it can be detected if there is a leak. If a gas leak is suspected, do not go searching for it with a lighted candle, match or lighter. Also, do not press any electrical switches, e.g. lighting, as a spark in the circuit inside the switch could ignite the gas fumes and cause an explosion.

8 Calor gas appliances should not be used as a form of heating in hairdressing or beauty therapy workplaces. They are an open flame fire and as such constitute a fire hazard, especially when coupled with the inflammable products in use.

Health and safety at work

The Health and Safety at Work Act 1974 applies to both employers and employees and demands that they take reasonable care for the health and safety of themselves, other staff, and people who are affected by their work, i.e. clients.

Every employer or manager responsible for five or more employees is required by law to write a health and safety policy for their business. This is a written evaluation of risk towards everyone (staff and public) on the premises for every aspect of work and the working environment. It should be shown that all risks and hazards have been identified and considered, eliminated, or minimised and controlled. A copy of this policy has to be given to each member of staff, ensuring that they read and understand it. The HSE supplies a booklet, *Writing a Safety Policy Statement: Advice to Employers* (Ref. HSC6), to help with writing this policy.

A written health and safety policy should cover such things as details of storage of chemicals; contents and layout of the stock cupboard; details of all electrical equipment checks; escape routes and evacuation procedures; name and address of key holders; the names of the persons responsible for first aid and health and safety; the location of the first-aid box and accident book; and a description of the management structure of the business, as well as other items peculiar to the profession (see also risk assessment, page 43).

Since 1974, regulations have been passed under the provisions of the Health and Safety at Work Act to ensure that every aspect of health and safety at work has been carefully thought about and legislated for. In this way, health and safety at work can be maximised. Examples of such regulations are COSHH and RIDDOR (see pages 24 and 122). A summary of the regulations is provided in Appendix 1, page 124.

Other legislation affecting the working premises includes:

- the Fire Precautions Act 1971 – see page 29
- the Office, Shops and Railway Premises Act 1963 (revised 1971) – see page 44
- the Data Protection Act 1984 – see record keeping, page 40.

HEALTH AND SAFETY CHECK LIST	Prepared by:			
Date:	Daily	Monthly	3/6/12 Monthly	Monthly

Salon Name:

Tick the appropriate box for when each check should be done.
Use a separate booklet to record and sign the check.

1. **Registration of premises** - notifying authority

2. **Written Health & Safety Policy Statement**
   Revision
   Attention of all employees

3. **Health & Safety Law** - Poster - displayed and conspicuous
   Addresses - displayed and conspicuous

4. **First Aid Kit** - Contents - No personal medications
   Accident Book

5. **"Appointed Persons"**, who?
   Allow for shiftwork, holidays, illness, leaving, etc.

6. **Fire fighting appliances.** Checking, siting, suitability.

7. **Emergency procedures,** doors, routes (internal/external).

8. **Thermometer,** displayed and condition.
   Heating systems, including portable.

9. **Welfare arrangements**
   Sanitary, maintenance, cleanliness, lighting
   Washing, maintenance, cleanliness, soap/towels. H/c, etc.
   Eating drinking facilities
   Rest periods, facilities

10. **Ventilation**
    Workroom(s), window openings, and/or mechanical extraction.
    Sanitary facility.

11. **Lighting,** artificial and natural, all areas
    (including stairs, passages, steps)

12. **Handrails to stairs,** condition, adequacy

13. **Handrails to steps,** condition, adequacy

14. **Furniture,** chairs, tables - condition, suitability, support, back,
    legs, feet.
    Cabinets (including filing cabinets, etc.) secure.

16. **Electrical.** V= Visual Check. AC= Approved Contractor
    Apparatus Hair   El.Lead   Plug.   Fuse Rating.
    i.e.Large dryers
    i.e.Portable dryers
    i.e.Tongs

    Apparatus Beauty
    i.e. Facial electrical machines

    i.e. Body electrical machines

ELLISONS ACADEMY A WORLD OF OPPORTUNITY

A health and safety checklist

	Daily	Monthly	3/6/12 Monthly	Monthly
Apparatus General				
Water heaters				
Vacuum cleaners				
Lighting				
Displays (inc. "counters")				
The Till				
Fixed system wiring				
Sockets				
Fuse board Markings/Identification and accessibility				
Records kept - updated.				
17. COSHH Assessment. Emergency procedures				
New substances to salon - assessment				
Training - new staff, casual staff (inc. holiday relief)				
Work placement/training				
18. **Consideration "Out of Hours" staff,** eg. cleaner(s)				
Training, first aid, reporting,				
COSHH, telephone contact, emergency line.				
19. **Provision of protective clothing** and protective means.				
20. **Public protection**				
Access and egress. Clothing. Personal possessions				
21. **Skin piercing work** - registration - byelaws, no smoking, records.				
22. **Public Liability Certificate** (Health & Safety enforcement).				
23. **Refreshments**				
Compliance with food hygiene regulations				
Registration				
Separate Bowls. "Wash Hands" sign				
Storage of food. Handling.				
24. **Telephone contracts**				
Emergency/reporting				
Listed, updated				
25. **Floor and surfaces.**				
Cleanliness				
Trip hazards				
Slip hazards, inc. "wet" flooring				
Changes of levels - conspicuous markings				
Mat wells				
Passage ways, unobstructed, lighting				
Head of stairways				
Wear & tear - floor coverings				
26. **Employees**				
Clothing. Personal possessions. Access/egress.				
27. **Schoolchildren** All under 16's ie. juniors need to be registered with local County Council.				

ELLISONS ACADEMY
A WORLD OF OPPORTUNITY

Immunisation

Workers handling needles frequently, e.g. electrologists, tattooists and acupuncturists, may feel happier with protection in the form of immunisation against hepatitis B. If so, your own family doctor should be consulted. However, current medical statistics show that hairdressing and beauty therapy workers in general are not more at risk from contracting this disease than the general population.

Insurance

• • • • • • • • DANGERS • • • • • • • •

A legal claim made against the salon which could result in very large financial losses and possibly sale of the owner's business and home; public prosecution and a fine for not carrying essential insurance cover, e.g. employer's liability insurance; damage occurring which the salon cannot afford to repair.

• • • • • • • PRECAUTIONS • • • • • • •

Employers and self-employed persons must, by law, hold **employer's liability insurance**. The Employer's Liability (Compulsory Insurance) Act 1969 places a duty on employers to take out insurance which indemnifies them against any legal liability to pay compensation to employees for bodily injury, illness or disease caused during the course of their employment. This insurance certificate is required by law to be displayed in the workplace for the employees to see. Employers must at present (1997) insure for at least £2 million per claim, but check with your insurance company.

Although not legally compulsory, it is strongly recommended that employers and self-employed persons should hold **public liability and product liability insurance** which indemnifies them against legal liability to pay compensation to third parties for bodily injury, illness or disease or loss or damage to property which arises in connection with their business.

Product liability provides insurance cover for the products used and should be carried by the manufacturers of the products. If well-known brands are always used, concern on the part of the hairdresser or therapist is minimised. If anything goes wrong due to the product, it should be the responsibility of the manufacturer of that product. However, the manufacturer may not be insured, or may have ceased trading, in which case the salon becomes responsible for any problems. This is why it is wise for a salon to carry its own product liability insurance.

Also strongly recommended is **professional indemnity and treatment risk insurance** which indemnifies employers and their staff against any costs arising from mistakes which they may make while giving professional advice or carrying out a professional treatment on a client.

TIP BOX

The signing of a disclaimer by a client *does not* excuse the professional person from responsibility in the eyes of the law should the treatment go wrong, e.g. piercing through an area of the body other than the soft fleshy part of the ear lobe, or carrying out a perm, colour or bleach on hair which has been previously treated with an incompatible product. Check with the salon insurers if you have any doubts about this.

TIP BOX

Regardless of whether the client says they are taking action or not, any accident or mishap must be reported to your insurance company immediately.

Self-employed persons should consider holding the following insurances:

- **Property owner's liability** (sometimes known as buildings insurance). A property owner would be advised to carry this insurance to guard against damage to the outside of the property, e.g. roof, slates, walls, etc. Internal fixtures, e.g. a toilet or a fitted kitchen, are usually covered by this insurance. Check that site clearance and architect fees are included in the rebuilding costs should the whole property

TIP BOX

Check with the insurers that external signs, neon signs and canopies are included in the insurance cover.

TIP BOX

Do not forget to notify the salon insurers of any changes to the premises or working practices, e.g. change of use of a room, erection of a new external sign, or the introduction of a new treatment.

be destroyed, e.g. by fire. Tenants should check in their lease if they or the property owner are responsible for this insurance.

- **Loss of earnings and staff wages.** This insurance covers loss of earnings if a fire or other catastrophe causes the workplace to be closed.
- **Personal accident or ill health.** This would also cover loss of earnings or pay an index-linked pension until retirement age if the insured were unable to work again, e.g. due to an accident to the hands or a severe viral infection.
- **Car insurance.** This is essential if stock or equipment is to be transported or a car used for mobile work (see page 38, mobile work).
- **Glass insurance.** Special cover for glass windows and mirrors.
- **Removable contents insurance.** Cover for the contents of the workplace, e.g. stock, tools, equipment and furniture.

TIP BOX

Many insurers will only provide contents insurance if burglar alarms, door and window locks, etc. are installed to their standards. Before installing any security devices, check with the salon insurers.

- **Legal expenses.** This insurance is taken out to cover the cost of any legal action taken by, for or against the salon, e.g. suing or unfair dismissal.
- **Temporary removal of property from the workplace.** Cover for equipment which has to be temporarily removed from the workplace, e.g. for repair.
- **Personal assault.** Cover in case of an attack while on the premises.

TIP BOX

For staff and personal safety, see Part One – Personal safety and security (pages 1–17).

- **Theft and burglary.** These terms mean different things to different insurers. Make sure you carry insurance for both and understand the difference.
- **Exhibition cover.** Check whether the exhibition hall demands that you carry your own public liability cover, and if so for how much. You could, for example, be liable for all costs if the hall burns down because of an electrical fault caused by you. Get extensions to your salon cover for exhibitions and negotiate cover for stock and materials, money and even personal accident while travelling.
- **Loss of rent.** Cover in case of an inability to pay through an accident or mishap, e.g. the premises burning down. Check with your lease whether you have to continue paying rent in this situation. This insurance can be held by the landlord or the tenant.

TIP BOX

Many of these minor points of insurance are covered in specialised all-risk policies or are negotiable extras. Simply check that they are all included.

Mobile work

See also pages 9 and 120.

• • • • • • • • DANGERS • • • • • • • •

Breakdown and assault, car and equipment theft, accident, limited sterilisation facilities, back strain through lifting.

• • • • • • • PRECAUTIONS • • • • • • • •

1   Select a car which allows you to lift equipment in and out easily, e.g. a hatchback, thus minimising the danger of back damage.
2   Make sure the car is serviced regularly.

TIP BOX

Use a garage which offers the loan of a car while yours is being serviced or repaired.

3   Join the AA, RAC or similar organisation for immediate help with a breakdown.
4   Carry a mobile phone to use in case of emergency, e.g. a car breakdown, accident, medical emergency, or physical danger. It is also advisable to carry a personal attack alarm, e.g. a Suzy Lampugh Trust Alarm (address on page 12), especially when taking money to the bank.

TIP BOX

Switch the mobile phone off while doing treatments on clients to ensure that they receive your full attention.

5   A business car will need to be insured for A1 fully comprehensive business use, and the insurance company must be told exactly what equipment is carried or left in the car. An extra premium will be required to insure this.
6   Special licences may be needed to carry out treatments at people's homes, e.g. massage, electrolysis, ear piercing, hairdressing, etc. Check with your local authority.
7   Sterilise the equipment at home or in the salon and place each set in a sealable new plastic bag which can be opened at the client's house.
8   Ensure that both public liability insurance (in case of damage to the client's home, clothing, etc.) and professional indemnity and treatment risk liability insurance (in case anything goes wrong with the treatments) are carried – see insurance, page 36.

TIP BOX

Mobile hairdressers and therapists need to exercise common sense as to the hours they work and the type of clients they take. Be aware that both sexes are open to allegations of rape, adultery or theft, as well as being vulnerable to attack, if they are on their own.

9 Always carry a first-aid box and a small, dry-powder fire extinguisher in your car.

10 Mobile workers should hold a current First Aid at Work Certificate.

11 Remember that volatile chemicals, e.g. essential oils, hair lacquer, bleach or nail products, can be a fire hazard. Ensure that precautions regarding ventilation, smoking and open fires are taken as in a normal workplace (see fire safety, page 29).

Overuse of hands

• • • • • • • • DANGERS • • • • • • • •

Repetitive strain injury (RSI or muscle overuse syndrome). This is the name given to a range of muscle, tendon and ligament injuries of the fingers, hands, wrists and elbows. It is caused by continuous repetitive or pressurised finger, hand or arm movements, e.g. continuous massage, application and filing of artificial fingernails, winding perms or normal rollers, and blow drying.

• • • • • • • PRECAUTIONS • • • • • • •

1 When sitting at a table to work, ensure that the table height is such that the hands are held more or less straight and not flexed up or down at a sharp angle. A firm foam pad on the table can be used to help support the wrists while working.

2 Take regular breaks during the day e.g. 10 minutes between each set of nail extensions or massage. Stretch or wriggle the hands during this period in order to use the hands in a different way.

TIP BOX

Anyone suffering from joint hypermobility (double jointedness) in the fingers and wrists is especially at risk from hand complaints. Heavy hand usage, e.g. massage and artificial nail extension work, should be avoided where possible.

3 If possible, spread the workload between a variety of jobs, not overloading on jobs known to cause strain.

4 Any pain, aching and tiredness of the wrists, arms, shoulders or neck during the working day is nature's sign that the body is doing too much and must rest. If these symptoms persist, especially if there is any persistent stiffness, heat or pain in the hands, wrists or finger joints, or even a loss of speed or accuracy, seek a doctor's advice and rest the affected areas.

5 Early rest leads to a cure. Neglect could lead to a lifelong incapacity.

Personal protective equipment (PPE)

• • • • • • • • DANGERS • • • • • • • •

Spillage on to clothes or body; splashes or objects going into the eyes; dangerous or reactive substances coming into contact with the hands; prosecution if adequate provision has not been made.

• • • • • • • PRECAUTIONS • • • • • • •

1 All employers must, by law, provide suitable protective equipment for their employees if this has been identified as being necessary following a risk assessment.

TIP BOX

Beware of cheap latex gloves. These can contain a protein that enters the body via cuts and can cause a strong allergic reaction. Always wash latex gloves before use, and if any users show signs of an allergic reaction (rashes, dizziness, etc.), seek medical help immediately.

2 This equipment has to be maintained, and staff must be trained to use it correctly. Employees are required to report loss of or damage to this equipment to their employer immediately so that it can be replaced or repaired.

3 In hairdressing and beauty therapy workplaces, protective equipment would include eye protection for use when mixing solutions, e.g. perms, bleaches, essential oils and lash tints, and when clipping artificial nails; masks for use

with sprays, volatile chemicals and powders/dusts, e.g. setting sprays for artificial nails, bleach, and artificial nail filing (especially when a drill is used); and gloves and other special clothing, e.g. aprons, for protecting the hands, body and clothing from reactive solutions or body fluids such as blood, vomit, perms, bleaches, essential oils, lash tints, strong disinfectants and sterilising solutions.

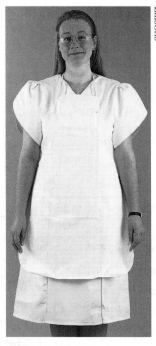

A beauty therapist's apron

TIP BOX

The employer has to provide the protective equipment and teach staff how and when to use it. After that, it is the responsibility of the hairdresser or therapist to ensure that they use the equipment as advised.

Record keeping

• • • • • • • • DANGERS • • • • • • • • •

If adequate records are not kept there is a danger of the insurance cover being invalidated, repeated allergy reactions, unsuccessful treatments, carrying out a treatment which is contraindicated, selling ineffective products, or being unable to contact a client in an emergency. There is also a danger of prosecution if the standard of record keeping does not comply with the Data Protection Act.

• • • • • • • PRECAUTIONS • • • • • • • •

The following items need to be kept on a client record:

1 The name, address and telephone number of the client so that they can be contacted if necessary, e.g. to cancel their appointment if the hairdresser or therapist is ill, to remind them of their appointment, to enquire why they have not kept an appointment and reschedule if necessary, to send details of promotions, or to inform them if the salon moves or changes its telephone number.

TIP BOX

Remember to record the title of the client, e.g. Dr, Mrs, Mr, Ms or Miss, as people can easily take offence if addressed incorrectly.

2 The name, address and telephone number of the client's doctor and next of kin in case they become ill while on the premises.

3 Any medical details, as these may contraindicate certain treatments. It is important that the client tells you if they suffer from certain complaints, e.g. epilepsy, varicose veins, pregnancy, high or low blood pressure, diabetes, arteriosclerosis, liver, heart or kidney disease, tuberculosis, thyroid trouble, cancer or breathing difficulties. If they are taking any medication this must also be recorded as it could be a contraindication to treatment. These details must be checked regularly, at least at the start of each new series of treatments, in case they have changed.

4 Precise details of any previous treatments carried out on the client, their effectiveness and whether any allergies were encountered. This gives a guide as to how to carry out or select future treatments and how to avoid unwanted reactions or outcomes.

TIP BOX

It is a nice gesture to give clients leaving your area a copy of their records. This can be passed on to their next hairdresser and therapist so that the continuity of treatments can be maintained.

5 The condition of the client or part of the client being worked on before the start of the treatment, e.g. bitten nails, dry hair or extremely nervous disposition. This could prove important if anything were to be questioned later.

STRICTLY PROFESSIONAL	BEAUTY TREATMENT

NAME

Date of birth.

Address.

Postcode.

Occupation.

Evening.

Phone Day.

Doctors Phone No.

Doctors name and address.

MEDICAL HISTORY

Notes.

Diabetes	Hypertension	Cold sores
Epilepsy	Headaches/Migraine	Moles
Heart condition	Asthema	Irregular skin pigmentation
Abnormal	Varicose veins	Prickly heat
Blood pressure	Verucca/Athletes foot	Number of children
Kidney	Fainting/Giddyness	Last pregnancy
Liver (esp. Hepatitis)	Hormone replacement	Others
Major operations	Very sensitive skin	
Hormone irregularities		

Allergies.

Are you under medical supervision
Are you taking any medication (esp. antibiotics, steroids, the pill)

FACIAL DIAGNOSIS

Notes.

SKIN TYPE	
Acne	Open pores
Oily	Blocked pores
Normal	Milia
Dry	Dilated Capillaries
Sensitive	Skin tags
Mature	Moles
	Dry patches

Eye area.

Neck area.

Recommended skin care routine and products

I have read and understood the details above.

Signed.

Dated.

A beauty therapy record card

CLIENT RECORD CARD				
Name:	Address:	Age group: ☐ 5–15 ☐ 16–30 ☐ 31–50 ☐ 50+		
Telephone numbers:	Date first registered:			
Home:	Stylist:	Skin type:		
Work:				
Hair condition:	Scalp:			Stylist
Date	Services used	Remarks		

A hairdressing record card

6 The dates and times of the treatments, again in case anything were to be questioned later.

7 The cost of the treatments, which gives an indication of client spending power.

8 Any retail products purchased, their type or shade, so that they can be bought again or avoided in future.

9 Other details, such as occupation and hobbies, which may have a bearing on certain treatments, e.g. nail extensions.

10 Personal details such as names of children or special pets. These are clearly not essential details, but if used in conversation they can make the client feel welcome.

Whether this information is stored on record cards in a filing system or on a computer database, record keeping comes under the legislation of the Data Protection Act 1984. The holder of the record undertakes not to pass this information on to anyone else without the express permission of the person involved. If a member of staff takes the names and addresses of their clients away from the salon, their behaviour is breaking the law and a prosecution could be brought against them under the terms of this Act. The contents of databases must *never* be sold on without the written permission of all the recorded people, as this would contravene the Act.

Under the Data Protection Act, anyone who holds personal data on computer has, by law, to be registered in order to do so. Registration costs £75 (1997) for three years, after which the the person must re-register. A registration pack is available from The Data Protection Registrar, Wycliffe House, Water Lane, Wilmslow, Cheshire SK9 5AF. Telephone 01625 545745. Note: it is expected that this legislation will be extended to encompass some types of manually kept records as from October 1998.

Computill Ltd

Computerised record keeping

TIP BOX

Insurance policies usually contain a clause stating that adequate records must be kept or the insurance will be invalidated. If the insurance company does not have access to adequate records and data regarding treatment of a client, it cannot fight any claim made against you by the client.

Reporting of Injuries, Diseases and Dangerous Occurrences Regulations (RIDDOR) 1995

These regulations cover the recording and reporting of certain serious accidents and conditions to the relevant authorities. They were mentioned in the section on fire safety and will be covered in detail in the fourth part of this book (page 122).

Risk assessment

• • • • • • • • DANGERS • • • • • • • •

Accidents can ruin lives, lower business output, damage premises and equipment, increase insurance costs and result in a court appearance. They may also lead to a damaged reputation and bad publicity. Prosecution may result if the necessary documentation is not kept available for inspection.

> **TIP BOX**
>
> A **hazard** means anything that can cause harm, e.g. chemicals or electricity. A **risk** is the chance, great or small, that someone will be harmed by the hazard.

• • • • • • • PRECAUTIONS • • • • • • •

Employers are required by law (The Management of Health and Safety at Work Regulations 1992) to make an assessment of any risks to the health and safety of employees and clients in the workplace, and to eliminate these risks as far as possible. Five steps are recommended in the regulations:

1 Look for any hazards.
2 Assess the risks of the hazards; decide who might be harmed and how.
3 Try to eliminate or control and minimise any hazardous or risky situations. (This will already have been done for any chemicals in use in order to comply with the COSHH regulations, see page 24.)
4 If you have more than five employees, you must record your assessment and actions. A form to

help you do this, called *5 Steps to Risk Assessment* is available from the HSE. Also available from the HSE and written by the Health and Safety Commission is a booklet called *Writing a Safety Policy Statement: Advice to Employers* (HSE6).
5 Review and revise your assessment as necessary, e.g. whenever changes such as new products, equipment, treatments or salon alterations are introduced, or simply every six months to take into account wear and tear, on floor coverings for example.

> **TIP BOX**
>
> Although five or more people have to be employed before written risk assessments and documentation are necessary by law, common sense dictates that this procedure should be carried out however many staff are employed. Many insurers require a written risk policy regardless of the size of the establishment.

> **TIP BOX**
>
> A current 'Health And Safety Law' poster must, by law, be displayed in the workplace for employees to see.

Skin care (dermatitis)

• • • • • • • • DANGERS • • • • • • • •

Occupational contact dermatitis, allergy.

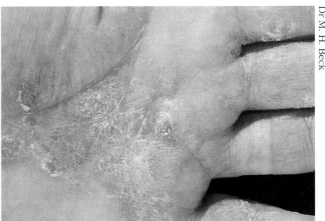

Dermatitis

Dr. H. Beck

• • • • • • • • PRECAUTIONS • • • • • • • •

1 If you are aware of the causes of skin problems, you will be able to take action to prevent them occurring. Skin problems are likely to be caused by:

- use of products carrying a skin hazard warning on their data sheets
- handling rough or abrasive products, e.g. scouring cloths/powders, spiky rollers or exfoliant creams
- getting the hands wet too often – this strips the natural protective oils from the skin
- not washing and drying the hands properly
- working with solvents (e.g. nail varnish remover), glues (e.g. nail glues), corrosives (e.g. bleach), and a variety of cosmetic products without adequate protection – reaction can be immediate, or occur after years of contact has produced a sensitisation reaction (allergy)
- allergy towards tools, e.g. nickel allergy from cuticle clippers or scissors
- contact with fine dusts and powders, e.g. acrylic powder, bleach, henna and nail filings
- extremes of temperature (especially for mobile workers) and humidity (water, saunas, steamers, foot and hand baths) in the workplace.

TIP BOX

By law (Office, Shops and Railway Premises Act 1971), the _minimum_ temperature allowed in the workplace should be 16°C within one hour of starting work. There is no stated maximum temperature. A thermometer must be displayed for staff to see.

2 Many skin problems can be prevented by being thorough with COSHH assessments, reading data sheets, finding out which products present a danger, and either finding and using less damaging products or providing personal protective equipment (PPE, e.g. gloves) for use with them.

3 Teach staff to recognise problems and insist that they see a doctor as soon as a problem develops, no matter how small. If skin problems are treated quickly, they can be cured. Left to establish, problems can soon become serious.

4 If one case of dermatitis occurs, see if anyone else has been affected. Look at working methods. Have any procedures changed? Have any new products been introduced, or old ones reformulated? Try to track down the causes and eliminate them.

5 Always make sure that adequate washing and drying facilities are available; that moisturising creams are available and used to replenish skin oils after washing at home as well as work; that barrier creams are available and used as directed to protect the hands (some only require application twice a day, even when shampooing is the main activity); and that good quality, comfortable gloves are always available and worn whenever necessary.

6 Avoid using hot-air hand dryers in staff kitchens and toilets. Apart from the hazard of increased bacterial growth in the warmed air which is taken from the floor area (see sterilisation, page 46), most people become impatient with the time taken to dry their hands using this equipment and so do not complete the process, leaving their hands damp and susceptible to skin problems.

TIP BOX

A pocket card, Occupational Contact Dermatitis (MS(B)6), is available free of charge from the HSE. Give copies to your staff to remind them of the dangers and precautions associated with skin care.

Skin testing

Although a vital part of salon routine, especially for insurance purposes, the limitations of skin tests must be understood. Women in particular are subject to rapid hormonal changes within their bodies due to the menstrual cycle, pregnancy and the menopause. Skin sensitivity varies enormously as the hormone levels fluctuate. A woman may have no reaction to a skin test one day, and yet the day after react severely to the treatment because she has, for example, started her period. The reverse is also true – she could react badly to a skin test one day, and yet be non-reactive 2–3 days later. This fluctuation in skin sensitivity can affect many treatments, e.g. waxing, aromatherapy, ultra-violet treatments, tinting and bleaching. Hairdressers and therapists must be aware of this at all times and avoid giving possible reactive treatments, e.g. tinting and hair removal by waxing, in the 2–3 days before and after menstruation, and during menstruation. Hairdressers should be aware of the possibility of unexpected results occurring during hair restructuring treatments, e.g. permanent waving, at this time.

TIP BOX

If the client reports an allergy to any substance, e.g. make-up or foods, this is an indication that they may be allergic to products used in hairdressing or beauty therapy treatments.

While men are not subject to such rapid fluctuations in hormone levels, skin testing for possible allergic reactions in them is equally important.

TIP BOX

Do not assume that because a client has been allergy tested for a product in the past, they will react the same way in the present.

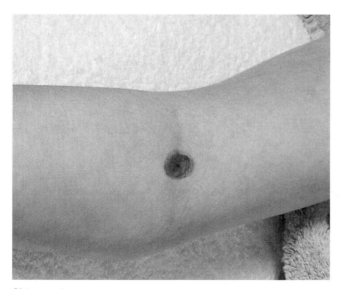

Skin testing

How to carry out a skin test

Carry out this test 48 hours before any possibly reactive treatment. Select a small area on the inside of the upper arm or behind the ear (the latter is the more usual site to choose). Carefully wash and dry the area to degrease the skin, and apply 2–3 drops of the solution to be tested. Make sure that the solution is the same strength as the one you propose to use during the treatment. Allow 2–3 minutes for the solution or cream to dry before wiping away the excess. Leave the area alone and uncovered for 48 hours. If, during this time, there is any itching, redness, blister or spot formation, then the treatment must not be carried out.

TIP BOX

Do not cover the area with a plaster – the client may be allergic to it.

Smoking

• • • • • • • • DANGERS • • • • • • • • •

Effects of passive smoking, discomfort to staff and clients, fire risk.

• • • • • • • PRECAUTIONS • • • • • • • •

1 From 1 January 1996 smoking must be prohibited in staff rest areas, or separate rest areas must be designated where smoking is allowed (Health, Safety and Welfare Regulations 1992).
2 Ideally, smoking should not be allowed in the workplace. To avoid offence, a sign could be displayed stating: 'Due to the inflammable nature of the chemicals used in our work, we request that clients do not smoke in the salon.'

TIP BOX

If no smoking rules are to be introduced, you must consult fully with all employees first so that amicable and workable agreements can be reached.

Sterilisation and disinfection procedures

• • • • • • • • • DANGERS • • • • • • • • •

Insufficient cleanliness, disinfection or sterilisation, leading to the spread of viral infections, e.g. hepatitis B or HIV in instances where the skin is damaged in any way; fungal infections, e.g. athlete's foot; bacterial infections, e.g. pustules, skin infections; and insect infestations, e.g. scabies, head lice.

• • • • • • • PRECAUTIONS • • • • • • •

I Basic to sterilisation techniques is a high level of general cleanliness in the workplace and among the staff. In addition to general hygiene, hairdressers and therapists should wash their hands in a recognised bactericidal cleanser before and after each treatment. The whole workplace should be washed and wiped or scrubbed down frequently with a disinfectant as well as a soapy cleanser in the washing water. There are many antibacterial disinfectant products available for use, ranging from concentrated liquids to sprays and effervescent tablets.

TIP BOX

Do not use hot-air hand dryers in the workplace. They draw up their air supply from the floor where bacteria gather, warm it, and push the warmed bacteria out into the general air circulation of the room.

TIP BOX

Always buy liquid soap in sealed dispensers and do not refill as bacteria can breed in the soap.

2 All equipment, e.g. brushes, combs, vibrator heads, vacussage cups, tweezers and scissors, must be scrubbed clean after every use with a soapy and/or solvent solution to remove grease and grime, then sterilised or disinfected in an appropriate way.

TIP BOX

To minimise the risk of allergic reactions, always protect your hands with gloves before immersing them in chemical cleaning agents.

3 All fabric items should be washed regularly in hot soapy water to which disinfectant in the recommended dilution has been added. (Towels should be washed after each client.) Where possible, disposables should be used, e.g. staff kitchen towels, sunbed headrests, and floor coverings in cubicles where people will be walking with bare feet.

4 Treatments which involve the use of equipment that may accidentally puncture the surface of the skin, e.g. tweezers, comedone extractors, razors, clippers, cuticle clippers and scissors, require specialist sterilisation procedures. These should destroy bacteria, spores, fungi and viruses (which are particularly difficult to destroy), and must eliminate any risk of transferring hepatitis B or HIV. Suitable methods include autoclaving, dry-heat oven systems and activated glutaraldehyde solutions. Each of these systems should be operated according to the manufacturer's instructions.

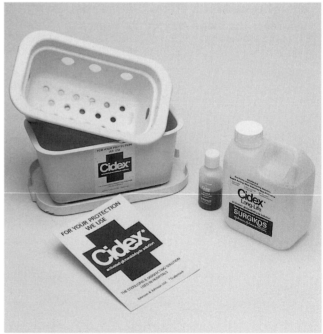

Sterilising equipment

Ellisons

TIP BOX

It has recently been found under testing that high-temperature glass bead 'sterilisers' do not give complete sterilisation.

5 The use of disposable equipment is essential wherever the skin is to be punctured as part of the treatment. Disposable electrolysis and acupuncture needles, ear-piercing systems which incorporate the use of a disposable gun, and disposable lancets are now widely and cheaply available. Electrolysis is a particularly high-risk treatment as far as infection is concerned, and disposables must be used. The old practice of ensuring that each client was allotted their own needle, which was sterilised between treatments but only ever used on that one client, is no longer believed to be completely safe.

TIP BOX

Sharp items, e.g. needles, have to be disposed of in special, safe, yellow, screw-topped sharps containers. When the container is full, it has to be disposed of using special disposal arrangements. Your local council offices (Environmental Health Department) will advise as to what these arrangements are. *Under no circumstances* put this waste with other general waste items.

TIP BOX

Many local health authorities insist on the use of a wide variety of disposable equipment, e.g. nail files and make-up brushes, and their use may soon become more widely enforced to avoid problems with, for example, hepatitis B.

6 For other equipment which is used externally to the body only, it is sufficient to use disinfection methods to rid them of bacteria, infestations and fungi. This type of equipment would include brushes, combs, vibrator heads, facial cleansing brushes, and make-up brushes.

TIP BOX

To guard against the entry of infection, always keep cuts covered.

7 As well as keeping equipment infection-free, materials also need to be considered. It is important to adhere strictly to application techniques as taught, e.g. taking a complete application of an item (such as a cleansing cream) from a jar with a clean implement and transferring it to the back of the hand or into a bowl for use from there, rather than returning time after time to an opened jar with an implement which could be contaminated after the first time it touched the client's skin.

8 After sterilisation or disinfection is complete, the equipment is only sterile or germ-free until its first encounter with air. All equipment should therefore be kept in a closed cabinet, e.g. a chemical vapour or ultra-violet cabinet, until its next use.

Sterilisation techniques

Disinfection is sufficient to kill the majority of bacteria, infestations and fungi, but sterilisation is needed to destroy viruses, spores and resistant bacteria and fungi. Suitable sterilisation techniques include autoclaving, dry-heat oven systems and activated glutaraldehyde solutions.

The necessity of an autoclave in hairdressing and beauty therapy workplaces is questionable if the above guidelines are followed and activated glutaraldehyde solutions or other suitable sterilising solutions are used according to specified guidelines. There may be a danger from hurried staff using the equipment incorrectly. However, where allergy to glutaraldehyde exists, an autoclave may be the only alternative. A fresh Total Sterilisation Test (TST) strip must be enclosed with each use to check that the sterilisation cycle has been carried through successfully, or an autoclave bought which indicates if sterilisation was successful.

Activated glutaraldehyde solutions take up to 10 hours (read the manufacturer's instructions) to sterilise submerged equipment, but disinfect within a few minutes. The solutions are toxic so the equipment needs to be removed with forceps and the solution rinsed off before use. The same solution can be used for up to 28 days (read the manufacturer's instructions) before it loses its effectiveness. However, constant use over this time is known to decrease its efficiency, and therefore its use as a sterilising agent is sometimes brought into question. Some people prefer to class it as a high-grade cold disinfectant. Dilute the solution before disposing of it down the drains.

TIP BOX

The equipment must be cleaned or washed to remove dirt and grease before placing it in the glutaraldehyde solution. Ensure that it is dried off thoroughly after washing so that the solution is not made ineffective by dilution.

TIP BOX

Keep a number of sets of all the equipment which needs to be sterilised so that some can be undergoing sterilisation while others are in use.

The COSHH data sheets for glutaraldehydes state that they can irritate the skin, eyes, throat and lungs. They can also cause sensitisation of the skin and respiratory tract. Once this has occurred, further exposure to even tiny amounts can cause dermatitis (allergic reaction of the skin), rhinitis and conjunctivitis (reactions of the nose and eyes, as in hay fever), and asthma (constriction of the airways). If this happens, the affected person will need to seek help from an occupational health doctor. Glutaraldehydes are a potential hazard and must be treated with respect:

- The occupational exposure standard is 0.2 parts per million.
- Glutaraldehydes should *not* be used as a general wipe-down disinfectant in the workplace.
- They should only be used in a well-ventilated area or preferably where there is proper ventilation equipment.
- Containers holding the diluted or concentrated solution should be kept covered.
- Gloves, apron and goggles should be used when handling the solution to avoid skin contact and splashes.
- Exposure to fumes from the solution should be avoided.

Storing clean equipment

Chemical vapour cabinets surround and impregnate the equipment with toxic chemical vapours. **Ultra-violet cabinets** surround the equipment with ultra-violet radiation. These

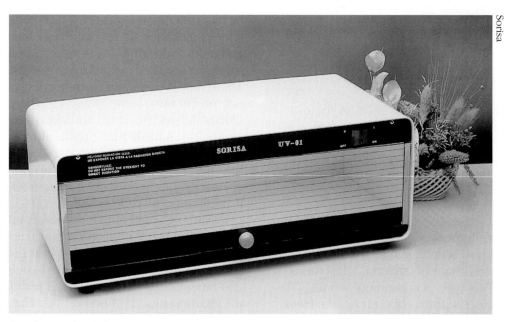

Sorisa

An ultra-violet cabinet

TIP BOX

Chemical vapour cabinets release toxic vapours into the air when opened, so care should be taken when using them. If buying a new system, the ultra-violet cabinet may be the safer option.

cabinets are used to store materials and equipment which have already been sterilised or disinfected in order to maintain their level of cleanliness. Hair and make-up brushes, cottonwool, nail buffers and sponges, for example, could be kept in one cabinet to maintain their bacteria-free status; while scissors, cuticle clippers, ear piercing guns and tweezers could be kept in a separate cabinet to maintain their sterile status.

Disinfecting jars containing quaternary ammonium compounds are useful for disinfecting and storing items of equipment in between their use. The solution needs changing daily and items which will rust should not be treated in this way.

Disinfecting jars

Safety in the beauty salon

Aromatherapy

Aromatherapy is the use of natural plant essences (essential oils) for healing and relaxation. In the salon situation, application is usually by massage (see page 67). Other methods are inhalation, vaporisation, in cosmetics or in the bath.

• • • • • • • • • DANGERS • • • • • • • • •

An adverse reaction to the oils used, e.g. ketone-containing essences such as fennel, rosemary, hyssop, wormwood and sage, can cause epileptic fits in prone clients. Saffron can cause convulsions, delirium and even death. Bergamot, lemon and lime can cause uneven skin pigmentation if applied before being exposed to strong sun or sunbed light. Cassia, clove, cinnamon and thyme are most likely to cause skin irritation. Many oils are toxic in large or small amounts. Only trained aromatherapists, knowing the medical history of their client and the qualities and dangers of the oils they are using, must practise aromatherapy.

• • • • • • • • PRECAUTIONS • • • • • • • •

1 An aromatherapist must *never* give or prescribe essential oils to be taken internally, e.g. by mouth or pessary. Such invasive treatment is the province of a medically qualified doctor or an aromatologist only (see the 1968 Medicines Act). Even if you think that you are suitably qualified, check with your salon insurance company to ensure that you have insurance for this type of treatment before administering it. **If insurance cover is not available, do not do it.**
2 **Essential oils** are pure oils extracted from natural plant material. They are up to 70 times more concentrated than the original botanical material and because of this, dosage is important. Used carelessly, they are likely to be poisonous. **Aromatherapy oils** are vegetable oils blended with essential oils or other aromatic compounds.

TIP BOX

An aromatherapist is qualified for the *external* use of essential oils on the body, while an aromatologist has extended their studies into the medical field and the *internal* use of essential oils.

TIP BOX

Always remember that if a claim is made against a salon, there may be difficulty in obtaining insurance renewal. It is recommended that aromatherapists, because they are working with people who are ill in various ways, should carry no less than £2 million of insurance cover.

3 Most oils keep their properties for only one year (lemon, orange and lime oils not even for as long as this), so make sure that they are bought from a reputable supplier with a fast turnover. The problem with buying 'off the shelf' is that there is no way of knowing how long the stocks have been there unless the bottle is date stamped; also the bottle seals may have been broken due to people trying and sniffing the oils before buying them.
4 In practice, due to the system-rebalancing effects and wide range of uses of each oil, an aromatherapist seldom uses more than 12–15 essential oils on a regular basis. Bearing in mind their limited shelf-life and potential toxicity, it is wise to stock only this number of oils. A suitable selection of oils might include lavender, juniper, camomile, rosemary, eucalyptus, geranium, a

citrus oil (e.g. bergamot), a melaleuca oil (e.g. tea tree), frankincense, rose, petitgrain, sandalwood, black pepper and clary sage. Most aromatherapists would agree that this selection of oils, adopted by the NVQ boards, is sufficient for most needs. Other oils may be added to this working list only after careful study of their properties.

5 Store essential oils upright, in dark glass bottles with efficiently sealed tops, in a cool, dark place. Oils deteriorate when in contact with light and air. Never use rubber tops, e.g. dropper bottles, for storage purposes as the vapours from the oil will rot the rubber and allow air to enter the bottle.

6 Essential oils are inflammable and as such must be treated and stored using the correct fire precautions for inflammable materials (see storage of chemicals, page 23).

TIP BOX

Use a dry-powder fire extinguisher for fires involving essential oils. Do not use water and be careful not to inhale smoke or fumes.

7 Some oils are toxic if swallowed, so all oils must be kept out of the reach of children.

8 Oils need to be mixed in non-reactive glass or porcelain containers. Separate droppers must be used to dispense each oil. If a dropper insert already exists inside the bottle, be aware that it may not be very accurate. Forcing the drop will give a small-sized drop, and often the drops run together in a 'flow', giving oversized drops. If you are using a dropper with a rubber or plastic bulb, do not draw the oil up into the bulb or it will be damaged and start to rot. Droppers can be cleaned by drawing up a little alcohol into the tube, flushing and repeating as necessary. Flush the residue down the sink with lots of water.

9 Essential oils are chemicals and, as such, safety precautions need to be taken when mixing and handling them (see PPE page 39). Eye shields, aprons and gloves must be worn, adequate ventilation provided, and industry codes of practice followed.

10 Barrier creams must be used on the skin before mixing and using the oils.

11 Hands must be washed thoroughly before and after mixing and/or using the oils, paying special attention if food is to be handled or consumed.

12 Due to their inflammable nature, smoking must not be allowed near the oils.

13 If spillage occurs, it should be cleaned up immediately using sand or an inert dry powder. Oils have been known to spontaneously combust and so tissues or fabrics which have been used to clean up any oils must be disposed of immediately, preferably by incineration. If oils spill on to clothing, it must be changed and laundered immediately.

14 Do not put oil containers directly on to polished surfaces, e.g. wood, as the oils will dissolve and mark the polish or varnish. Take care when handling glass bottles with oily hands.

TIP BOX

Because of the unpredictable effect of oils on individual clients, it is wise to give a patch test before treatment, especially where previous skin or other allergies are known. Note that certain drugs, stress and the menstrual cycle can affect sensitivity.

15 When using essential oils in burners or vaporisers, bear in mind how volatile and inflammable they are. Never allow the oil near a naked flame, and do not let the bowl of the vaporiser dry out while the candle is still alight. Place the burner on a firm, heatproof, level surface away from curtains, children and animals, and where it cannot be knocked over. Do not leave it unattended. Before lighting the candle, float 3–6 drops of oil on the water in the bowl. Put the oil away and *then* light the candle. To refill, first blow out the candle and allow the bowl to cool. Add water, then oil to the bowl, put the oil away and relight the candle.

16 When using a light-bulb ring, make sure that the lamp is in a safe place where it cannot be knocked over. With the bulb off and cold, place the ring on top of it, channel side up. Add water to the ring plus 2–3 drops of oil. Switch on the light. To refill, first switch off the light and allow

it to cool. Add more water, then more oil, and switch on the light again. **Cold water spilled on to a hot bulb could cause it to shatter and explode.**

17 When using essential oils in the bath, add about 6–8 but no more than 10 drops in total to a fully run bath (with children use 1–2 drops only). The oils can be blended first with a little vegetable oil or full-fat milk to aid dispersion (this must always be done with children).

TIP BOX

Essential oils can mark plastic baths if not dispersed properly. Wipe down plastic baths immediately after use.

---

18 When using essential oils in inhalations, make sure that the bowl is on a level, firm surface. Pour boiling water into 3 drops of oil (in total). The head is bent over the bowl and covered with a towel to retain the vapours. The mouth should be kept open to avoid scalding the nasal passages, and the eyes kept closed to avoid oil vapours entering them. Five minutes is sufficient for treatment, and extra care should be taken with asthmatics or hay fever sufferers.

19 When using essential oils to rinse hair, add 1–2 drops only to the rinsing water and disperse well. Take extreme care that the rinsing water does not go into the eyes.

20 When using essential oils in massage, do not use more than 5–6 drops of oil (in total) to every 10 ml of carrier oil (3%). With children, no more than 2 drops to 10 ml (1%) must be used. The rule 'less is more' applies with essential oils, many of them having an almost homoeopathic effect.

TIP BOX

Never give an aromatherapy massage treatment prior to the client having a sauna, sunbed session or hair treatment, as the heat intensifies the actions of the oils and may give unpredictable results.

---

21 Do not sell or give your own blended oils to your clients unless you carry product liability insurance (an expensive insurance usually only carried by manufacturers of products, see page 36). If anything goes wrong, the fault lies with the person making the product – you! Be safe and only sell products from a reputable manufacturer. Giving the client the leftover oils from the treatment is not as innocent as it seems. Do not do it!

22 Full and accurate records must be kept of every client and treatment. As well as being necessary to provide safety and continuity of treatment, failure to do this will invalidate insurance cover.

23 If any oils are swallowed, do not try to make the person sick, but seek medical attention immediately. If they enter the eye, flush thoroughly with cold water for 10 minutes and seek medical attention. See Part Three, First aid in the salon, for more thorough advice.

• • • • • • CONTRAINDICATIONS • • • • • •

Contraindications to treatment with aromatherapy include severe circulatory disorders, high or low blood pressure, a history of thrombosis or embolism, epilepsy, diabetes, nervous disorders, electronic implants, heart valve disorders, recent haemorrhage or swelling, inflammation, severe bruising, skin disorders, cuts, abrasions, recent scars, warts, moles, loss of tactile sensation, loss of the sensation of hot and cold, allergies (especially to perfume) and intolerances. Massage should not be applied over varicose veins, or over the stomach area if pregnant.

Where contraindications exist, or the client has any condition which causes doubt in the mind of the aromatherapist (e.g. cancer or pregnancy), written medical permission must be obtained before a treatment is carried out.

It is vital that the aromatherapist has in-depth knowledge of the oils and keeps this knowledge up to date. For example, at present aromatherapists consider it wise not to use aniseed, basil, birch, cedarwood, clary sage, cypress, fennel, hyssop, jasmine, juniper, marjoram, myrrh, nutmeg, parsley, peppermint, rose, rosemary, sage and thyme on anyone who is pregnant, even after they have obtained medical permission to carry out a treatment on her. This list is always being extended as more is discovered about the oils.

It is thought by many that aromatherapy cancels out the effects of homoeopathic treatment, so if the client is also seeing a homoeopath, their permission should be sought before treatment is undertaken.

Black skin

• • • • • • • • DANGERS • • • • • • • • •

Disguised sensitivity, keloid formation (lumps of skin tissue forming at the site of wounds), loss of pigmentation.

• • • • • • • • PRECAUTIONS • • • • • • • •

1 Take extra care when applying cosmetics or hair preparations of any kind to black skins. This is because black skins have a tendency to be more sensitive and prone to allergies than white skins, and any reactions which occur cannot be seen easily or quickly due to the masking effect of the skin colour.

2 Black skins are three times more likely to develop keloids than white skins. Because of this, it is important to be extra cautious when applying any treatment which might possibly cause tiny injuries as these may result  in keloid formation. Be particularly aware of this danger when carrying out ear piercing, electrolysis or pustule extraction on black clients.

3 Take care when applying electrical treatments, e.g. faradism or galvanism, to black skins, as they are more resistant to electrical currents than white skins.

Body wrap slimming techniques

• • • • • • • • DANGERS • • • • • • • • •

Interfering with the blood circulation (especially to the feet and lower legs, hands and lower arms), falls, cracked ribs, shortness of breath.

• • • • • • • • PRECAUTIONS • • • • • • • •

1 Do not wrap too tightly. As long as the body shows impression lines at the end of the treatment, there is no need to make the client feel thoroughly uncomfortable by wrapping tighter.

2 Do not wrap as tightly over the rib cage. Too tight a wrap here could result in an inability to breathe properly and even a cracked rib if the client sneezed.

3 Do not wrap tightly into the popliteal space behind the knee, or to the inner elbow area. There is no protection for the blood vessels here and it is in this area where the greatest risk of stopping the circulation occurs.

4 Do not wrap too tightly over varicosities. Although a varicose condition is only a contraindication to body wrap in advanced cases (firm bandaging is actually part of the treatment for varicose veins), affected areas must only be wrapped firmly, not tightly.

5 Ensure that the client has a handrail to hold on to during the wrapping procedure. The tugging, coupled with the muscular restriction once the client's legs have been bound, could easily lead to a bad fall.

6 Wash and dry the bandages between each treatment. If clingfilm or saran wrap is used, it should be disposed of preferably by incineration.

• • • • • • CONTRAINDICATIONS • • • • • •

– pregnancy
– advanced varicose veins
– skin infections or contagious conditions
– open cuts and sores (the gel stings quite severely)

People who have asthma, epilepsy or diabetes must not be given this treatment without a suitable letter of permission from their doctor. Even if they have this permission, a close watch must be kept on them during treatment and they must be unwrapped immediately if any untoward symptoms occur.

Clothing

• • • • • • • • DANGERS • • • • • • • • •

Falls, insufficient protection against allergies, burns, scalds and cuts.

• • • • • • • PRECAUTIONS • • • • • • • •

1 A protective overall, offering good coverage, should be worn to protect the beauty therapist from spillage of any harmful liquids.

2 Choice of shoes is important. As well as being comfortable, they should be flat and have non-slip soles to help prevent falls in the salon. Lace-ups are not to be recommended as these can lead to falls if the laces are not correctly tied. The shoes need to protect the feet against spillage of hot liquids or chemicals: sandals should definitely be avoided.

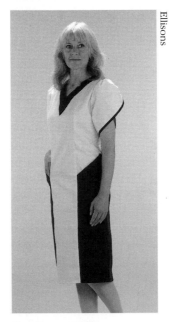

A salon overall

3 Scissors, cuticle clippers and knives must be kept in protective cases when not in use, not loose in pockets. This will avoid the possibility of accidental cuts.

4 Rubber gloves must be worn for any treatments where bleeding is a potential hazard, e.g. electrolysis, and for the handling of chemicals, e.g. bleach, essential oils and cleaning materials.

5 Clients must be adequately covered to protect them and their clothes from spillage of liquids or chemicals.

Ear piercing

See also page 105, ear-piercing infections and complaints.

• • • • • • • • • DANGERS • • • • • • • • •

Fainting, minor shock, keloid formation, tearing the ear lobe, skin burn, post-treatment infection. Ear piercing is a minor surgical operation and must be conducted in scrupulously clean and hygienic conditions.

• • • • • • • PRECAUTIONS • • • • • • • •

1 Make sure that the client is safely seated before the treatment commences. There should be no sharp edges, e.g. table corners, against which the client could fall if they faint.

2 Clip the client's hair back and bathe the area of the ear well with sterile medical swabs or wipes. At this stage, take note of the state of cleanliness of the client's hair, ears and skin. If any of these are dirty, tactfully point this out to the client as being a potential source of infection once the ears are pierced. Dirty ear canals can be cleaned *carefully* using cotton buds and the client should be advised to do so at home.

TIP BOX

The use of surgical spirit on the skin is no longer advocated because of possible reactions to it. Use a proprietary medical swab or wipe and aftercare solution so that the onus of product liability lies with the manufacturing company, not yourself.

3 The position of the stud must be marked with a special skin-marking pen. Any other type of pen could cause a toxic or allergic reaction. Once marked, check with the client if the positioning is correct before proceeding with the piercing. Do not forget to scrub your hands and nails with a medicated soap before touching the ear-piercing gun. Some therapists choose to wear disposable surgical rubber gloves while carrying out the treatment.

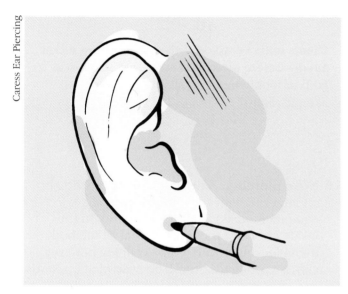

Caress Ear Piercing

Marking the client's ear prior to piercing

4 If the ear is to be repierced, try not to pierce over the previous scar tissue – this does not heal as quickly as normal skin tissue.

5 The client should be told what is happening at all stages of the procedure. Talk to them to put them at their ease. If you carry out the treatment without warning, the client might 'jump' when the stud is shot through the ear, possibly tearing the lobe as the stud is still positioned in the gun at this stage.

6 Aftercare instructions must be given verbally and in writing. Recommend a proprietary, specifically formulated aftercare solution. Do not tell the client to use liquid antiseptics – they may use the antiseptic in an undiluted state and extremely nasty skin burns can result from this. Creams of any kind must not be used on the area.

7 Clients must be given the following information and instructions for the aftercare of their pierced ears:

- Always wash your hands before touching the studs or surrounding area.
- Bathe the area with the recommended solution on cottonwool, front and back, morning and night, for a minimum of six weeks. After bathing, the front of the stud must be turned twice to keep it loose in the ear.
- The stud must not be removed for six weeks, and then it must be replaced with a solid gold one for wearing all the time. The client must not go without earrings for twelve months as the hole can heal up overnight during this time.
- Long hair must be kept tied back and all hair kept spotlessly clean.
- The use of hairsprays, colours, etc. in the area must be avoided until complete healing has taken place.
- Children must be told in very simple language the importance of cleaning the ears and not touching them themselves or letting friends touch them in between the cleansing times. (Parents must be instructed in the aftercare of their child's ears so that they can take responsibility for this.)
- The use of cheap earrings must be avoided at all times.

TIP BOX

As with any salon treatment, proper records must be kept detailing the name and address of the client, the date of treatment, and any comments regarding the treatment.

8 The client should be instructed to return to the salon immediately if any negative symptoms develop, e.g. redness or soreness.

9 Repeated piercings up the side of the ear can be fashionable. It is your duty to point out that the after-pain will be greater than when the piercing is done in the standard, fleshy, relatively nerveless lobe area. However, no harm will be done by piercing higher up the lobe as long as the piercing does not involve cartilage. Damage to cartilage does not heal as quickly because of its poorer blood circulation. If it becomes infected, the infection can pass to the surrounding bone and this then becomes very dangerous and difficult to clear up.

TIP BOX

Check with your insurance company what areas of the body are covered for piercing. Standard policies stipulate piercing is only to be done in the fleshy lobe area of the ear. Asking the client to sign a disclaimer before piercing other areas of the body is no protection against the client effectively suing at a later date should anything go wrong. Carrying out a treatment against your professional judgement is entirely your responsibility. Quite simply, do not do anything for which insurance cover is not available.

10 Do not repierce or multi-pierce a client who has a tendency to form keloids. This will only result in more keloids forming in the pierced area.

11 Babies are often brought in to have their ears pierced. Be well prepared so that the two studs can be shot through the ears within seconds of one another, i.e. in the space of time it takes the child to realise that it has been hurt. Pierce the ear which is most difficult to reach first, i.e. the one nearest to the parent holding the child. Also, pierce a little higher up than normal as the level of the hole tends to drop as the child grows. Make sure that the parent understands the aftercare instructions.

12 Never pierce ears with previously used studs. These are unsterile and there is an extremely high chance of infection occurring if they are reused. The gold coating will also be worn away, raising the chances of a metal allergy occurring. The system of charging only for the ear-piercing service, and providing new sterile earrings free, eliminates any argument along these lines.

13 In between treatments, the ear-piercing gun should be sterilised and kept in sterile conditions. Disposable systems should never be reused.

14 Ear-piercing studs should be purchased in sterile packets. Do not open these until you are ready to carry out the treatment. If you are using a gun system, load the gun directly from the package so that the ear studs are not touched or contaminated in any way.

15 If any discomfort lasts for more than 24 hours, or excessive redness, swelling or infection occurs, a doctor should be consulted.

TIP BOX

Clients must be asked if they suffer from nickel allergy before piercing. Nickel-free studs, e.g. gold or niobium, are available to use on allergic clients.

16 **Nose piercing.** Although fashionable, do not attempt this with standard ear-piercing equipment: making an open wound on the inside of one of the dirtiest areas of the body, then blocking it with a dirt-retaining butterfly clip, is inviting disaster. True nose-piercing studs are corkscrew shaped and utilise their own method of piercing. Under no circumstances should any technique other than this be carried out on the nose area. Do not attempt nose piercing unless you have received full training in the procedure and are insured to carry it out.

17 **Body piercing.** Body piercing is a surgical operation done using cannulas and other special piercing equipment. Again, do not attempt it unless full training has been received and you are fully insured to carry out the procedure. Disclaimers are not sufficient protection should anything go wrong.

• • • • • • CONTRAINDICATIONS • • • • • •

– Do not pierce through ear lobes which are too thick to allow the earrings to fit comfortably. Allow for swelling of the tissues.

– Never pierce inflamed lobes, even when the inflammation is temporary due to the wearing of clip-on earrings. Ask the client to remove the clip-ons and return when the redness has abated.

– Do not pierce through cysts, hard lumps, previous scar tissue or moles.
– Do not pierce through cartilage.
– Do not pierce if the client is suffering from rheumatic, heart or thyroid conditions or internal infections.
– Clients who have epilepsy or diabetes must have a companion with them.
– Do not pierce the ears of a child under the age of 18 without written parental permission.
– Acne sufferers and diabetics are slow to heal.
– If in doubt, don't pierce.

Electrolysis

• • • • • • • • DANGERS • • • • • • • • •

Electrolysis involves piercing the skin with a needle and possible blood-to-blood contact. To minimise the danger of infection, the rules of hygiene must be strictly followed (see sterilisation and disinfection procedures, page 46). Surgical rubber gloves must be worn by the operator and used needles disposed of safely in sharps containers. Other potential dangers include burns and scarring.

• • • • • • • • PRECAUTIONS • • • • • • • •

Short-wave method

1 Make sure that the angle of insertion is correct and that your working position enables you to achieve this easily. If the follicle wall is pierced, subcutaneous tissue will be destroyed. Enter the follicle from beneath the hair, not above it.
2 Make sure that the needle is inserted at the correct depth. Too deep a probe will destroy the subcutaneous tissue; too shallow a probe will burn the surface layers of the epidermis.
3 Use the lowest possible current which will remove the hair successfully. Too high a current will cause a heat burn, with resulting increase of pigment or an indentation of the skin.
4 Turn on the current only when the needle is fully inserted in the follicle. Inserting the needle with the current switched on will burn the surface layers of the epidermis and cause an indentation. Extracting the needle with the current on will leave a blister on the surface of the skin.
5 Do not work on hairs which are too near to one another. A healing gap must be left to prevent infection of nearby follicles.

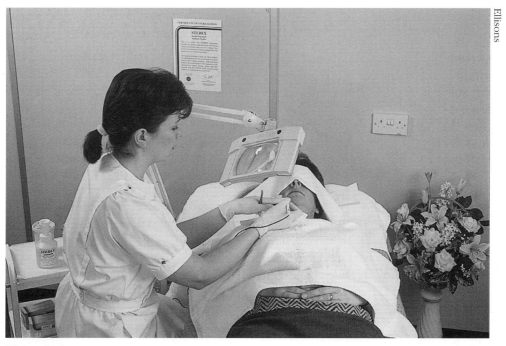

Electrolysis

6 Do not work for too long at a time: 50–60 minutes followed by a 15-minute break is an efficient working pattern. Any longer than this will lead to deterioration of technique and increases the danger of mistakes occurring.

7 Always use straight, sharp, disposable sterile needles.

8 Do not use too high a current on black skins as these are more likely to form keloids and will scar easily. To minimise this risk, always ensure that the first treatment starts with the lowest current strength recommended by the manufacturers of your particular machine. The strength can then be safely increased as necessary.

9 Always give the client verbal and written aftercare instructions and check that these are followed correctly.

10 In light of current knowledge regarding sterilisation and transmission of infection, all needles must be disposable and only used once.

Galvanic method

All the precautions previously given for the short-wave method also apply to the galvanic method. However, the current used is not as high so the risk of a heat burn is not as great as long as the correct technique is applied. The main risk is that of a chemical burn occurring under the skin due to the over-production of sodium hydroxide in the follicle.

1 Time the duration of the needle in the follicle very carefully. This is linked to the production of sodium hydroxide.

2 Keep a constant watch on the milliampere meter for any sudden increase in current due to the breakdown of skin resistance.

3 Make sure that the needle holder is attached to the negative pole. Hard, blackened scar tissue would result if it were attached to the positive pole.

4 Also follow the general precautions laid down for the use of galvanic current on the body (see page 62).

The blend method

As the blend utilises a mixture of galvanic and short-wave currents, all the precautions given in the two preceding sections apply. The two currents are used on very much lower intensities for this method, so the risk of damage is reduced. However, all

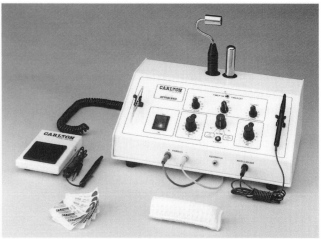

A blend epilation unit

precautions must still be strictly followed at all times.

High-frequency tweezer method

1 Do not search for a hair with the current switched on. Make sure that the foot pedal is only depressed while a hair is being held.

2 Do not work for too long at a time. One hour is long enough. After this, concentration begins to fade and will lead to operator error – the only real danger with this type of equipment.

• • • • • CONTRAINDICATIONS • • • • • •

All methods of electrolysis are contraindicated in the following circumstances:

– epilepsy, asthma, heart abnormalities or high blood pressure – the stress of the appointment, the overhead light or the radiation waves could trigger off an attack

– diabetes, as the poor skin-healing powers of diabetics can cause problems

– severe cases of varicose veins – if the tweezers or needle slipped, they could easily puncture a vein and cause severe bleeding

– moles, warts and any lumps – the absorption of high-frequency waves in these areas over any length of time, or simply the interference with the area, could cause it to turn malignant

– anyone with an infectious or contagious skin disease – there is a risk of spreading the client's complaint to the therapist or to other clients

– children under 18 years of age – time must be given for a child's hormone balance to settle down. Any superfluous hair appearing before this time can disappear spontaneously once puberty is passed. It is best to bleach the offending hairs up to this time

– under the arm or on the breast area if the client is suffering from mastitis (infection of the milk glands in the breasts)
– on the eyelids or any part of the eyebrow below the brow bone – one slip in this area could mean blindness for your client. It is also a very sensitive area and one most likely to react adversely to any form of treatment
– anyone with a cardiac assistor or pacemaker – the high-frequency waves can disrupt the workings of such a device
– in severe cases of acne, as infective complications and scarring can occur.

A well-qualified electrologist may carry out treatment on any of the above, but such treatment must be undertaken only at the written request of a doctor, under strict medical supervision, and with extreme caution being exercised at all times. It must not be attempted in any other circumstances.

Exercises

• • • • • • • • DANGERS • • • • • • • • •

Overcrowding or insufficient space causing danger of physical injury to the therapist, the client or other clients; fainting; cramp; hyperventilation; extreme fatigue; muscle damage; failure of apparatus.

• • • • • • • PRECAUTIONS • • • • • • • •

1 Do not allow exercising in confined spaces, too near apparatus, or with clients too close together. Allow at least two square metres for each client.
2 Make sure that there is an adequate supply of fresh air and that the temperature in the room does not become too hot. In cases of freak hot weather, the exercises should be modified accordingly.
3 A careful watch should be kept on each client who is exercising. If it is a large class, teach from a raised platform so that this is possible. Each group of exercises should be adaptable to three

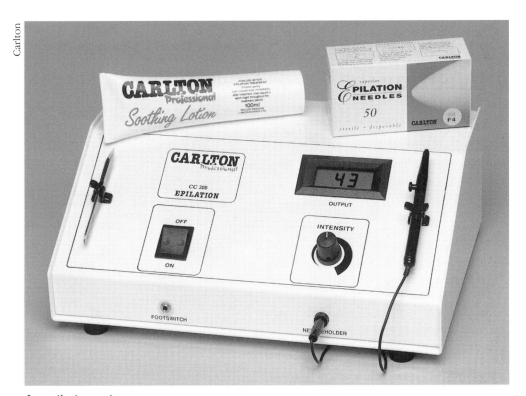

Carlton

An epilation unit

levels – beginner, intermediate and advanced. Under no circumstances should a client be allowed to exercise past their own level. This applies equally to breathing exercises.

4 No exercise session should begin without an extensive warming-up sequence to stretch and prepare the muscles for more strenuous movements. Starting an exercise session without warming up is inviting muscle damage.

5 All apparatus should be checked daily by the therapist and frequently (at least twice a year) by a maintenance engineer.

• • • • • • CONTRAINDICATIONS • • • • • •

Any person receiving medical attention or treatment should not be allowed to join an exercise class of any kind unless written permission has been obtained from a doctor or specialist. The instructor or supervisor must take care to ask new clients about their general health and should display a notice asking them to inform her if they suffer from any of the following conditions: obesity, muscular problems, back conditions, heart complaints, high or low blood pressure, diabetes, epilepsy, headaches, fainting spells, pregnancy, recent operations or childbirth, previously broken bones. Exercises can then be modified to suit each client and a careful watch kept on anyone liable to experience any difficulty. Records must be kept as appropriate.

Eyebrow tweezing

• • • • • • • • DANGERS • • • • • • • • •

Tiny nips and cuts may be inflicted on the client during this treatment unless care and concentration are exercised at all times. To minimise the dangers of infection and blood-to-blood contact as a result of both this and the removal of hairs from their follicles, the rules of hygiene must be strictly followed (see sterilisation and disinfection procedures, page 46). Surgical rubber gloves may be worn by the operator as a precaution.

The client will not be very pleased if a cut does occur as it will be in a prominent position on the face. Always inform your client of any damage inflicted, no matter how small.

• • • • • • • PRECAUTIONS • • • • • • • •

1 Stretch the area of skin to be worked upon between the first and second fingers of the hand not holding the tweezers.

2 Use tweezers with tips machined to an angle instead of straight across. This helps to prevent loose skin being caught by the corner of the tweezers nearest to the skin.

3 Take extra special care on clients whose skin has a tendency to wrinkle (crêpe-like). Accidental nips are most likely to occur on this type of skin. Stretch it well between the fingers.

4 Wipe the area with a proprietary wipe or antiseptic-soaked cottonwool pad, both before and at frequent intervals during the treatment. This helps to eliminate the risk of infection if an accident does occur. It also has a soothing, cooling action on the tweezed area.

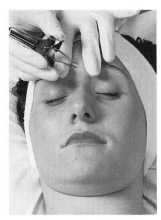

Tweezing at the bridge of the nose

Eyelash and brow tinting

• • • • • • • • DANGERS • • • • • • • •

Burns and allergic reactions.

• • • • • • • • PRECAUTIONS • • • • • • •

1 Make sure the peroxide is not too strong: 10 volume is more than adequate for mixing with the tint. Do not use too much peroxide as this will result in a 'runny' tint which may seep into the client's eyes.

2 Keep away from the eyes. Only a smear of tint is necessary to obtain colour.

3 Protect the surrounding skin

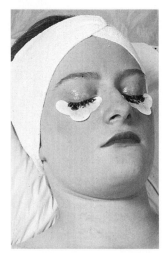

Eyelash tinting – protect the surrounding skin

area with petroleum jelly and a lint or paper under-eye pad also smeared with petroleum jelly.

4 Always give the client strict instructions not to open the eyes until told to do so.

5 Take care not to over-process the hair. Always read the instruction leaflet provided with the tint to obtain the correct application time. This will vary from product to product.

6 Always administer a skin test 48 hours in advance to ensure that no allergy is present. Keep a record of this for future reference, but repeat the test before every consecutive treatment. Allergies can arise spontaneously where there has been no previous reaction and the allergy can be due to either the peroxide or the tint. Because of this, it is essential to carry out a skin test even when you are using vegetable-based tints (see page 45).

7 Do not apply lash tint to a client wearing contact lenses – the tint could seep under the lenses and cause extreme irritation and burning of the conjunctiva.

8 Make sure that all the tint has been removed from the lashes with damp (not wet) cottonwool pads before instructing the client to open their eyes.

9 Never leave a client during treatment, so that you can keep a careful watch for their eyes watering. If this happens and the tint enters the eye and begins to sting, remove the tint immediately and apply the appropriate first aid (see page 106). Note: overhead lights are often a cause of eyes watering. Switch them off if possible.

10 Brows absorb tint much quicker than lashes and therefore need a shorter processing time. Do not darken naturally dark brows prior to sun exposure as they could then turn orange in the sun due to the effect of the peroxide in the tint.

• • • • • • CONTRAINDICATIONS • • • • • •

– any evidence of recent irritation in the eye, e.g. from swimming in chlorinated water
– any present or recent eye infection

Faradic units

• • • • • • • • DANGERS • • • • • • • • •

Electric shock; minor shocks from current sensation; rashes from sweating; over-treatment; allergy to the rubber pads; muscle exhaustion.

• • • • • • • • PRECAUTIONS • • • • • • • •

1 Always check that the intensity dials are at zero before switching on. Also check the surge interval, surge length, single or dual polarity, and the frequency of the current. Adapt these to your client to give a comfortable treatment.

2 During their placement, quickly check each pair of pads to see if they are passing the correct charge.

3 Always increase the current very slowly up to contraction. If it is a new client, explain the sensations to them as you are doing so, e.g. 'At first you will feel a gentle tingling sensation as the tiny current starts to flow. This will pass away as the muscle starts to move and contract. You should not feel any pain at all. If you do, you must tell me straight away.'

4 Do not allow the client to touch the machine – keep the controls out of reach.

5 Time the treatment carefully. Range the timing from 15 minutes for cases of post-operation or post-natal treatment to 45 minutes for regular clients – provided that medical permission has been given.

6 If the rubber causes an allergy reaction, place damp sponge pads between the rubber pads and the skin.

7 Always make sure that the pads are moistened to provide good contact with the skin. Ensure also that sufficient strapping is used to give the pads good contact. If they do not make good contact, unpleasant current sensation will result, and minor shocks will be felt.

8 Do not allow the client to move around during treatment as this will result in minor current shocks.

9 Check the wires and visible connections regularly.

10 After the treatment, always dry the client and apply a dusting of talcum powder to dry the skin completely and leave the client feeling comfortable. Only use unperfumed talcum powder on a client, as the perfumed varieties could cause an allergy reaction.

• • • • • • CONTRAINDICATIONS • • • • • •

– open cuts – cover with petroleum jelly
– varicose veins
– muscle disease
– pregnancy
– after childbirth, or any operation, until the

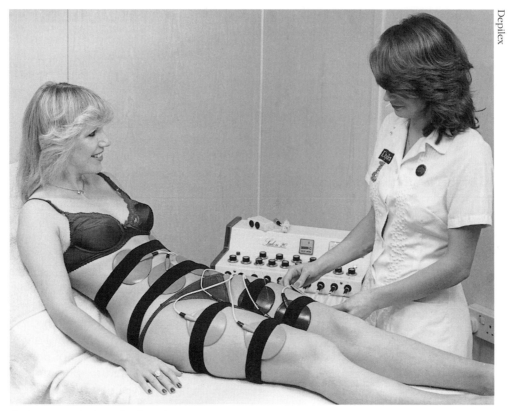

A client padded up for faradic treatment

doctor's permission has been given
- high blood pressure
- heart conditions
- copper interuterine devices
- pacemakers

If in doubt, e.g. with clients who have epilepsy or diabetes, seek medical advice and permission.

Galvanic current for facial and body treatments

• • • • • • • • • DANGERS • • • • • • • • •

Electric shock, burns (chemical, electrical and heat burns), allergic or sensitivity rashes.

• • • • • • • • PRECAUTIONS • • • • • • • •

1 Never allow the client to touch the machine – keep the controls out of reach.
2 Do not allow the electrodes to break contact with the skin while the current is flowing as this would cause it to jump the gap, spark and burn. Never use cracked electrodes as they do not maintain good contact with the skin. For body work, sheets of rubber impregnated with graphite are now available, which can be cut to size to make extremely flexible large electrodes. They are less liable to crack and maintain very good body contact. Spontex covers are still needed with this new type of electrode.
3 The therapist and client must remove all jewellery, watches and metal objects before treatment starts, otherwise the current will be attracted to the metal and cause a burn.
4 For each new client, an initial check for skin sensitivity should be made with a pin and cottonwool so that too much current is not inadvertently given to the client due to insensitivity on their part.
5 The client should be settled into a couch. It is important that the client is not in contact with any metal objects or moisture. These would give the current an opportunity to earth itself and cause a burn in this area. It is a good idea to have a rubber sheet covering the couch (but

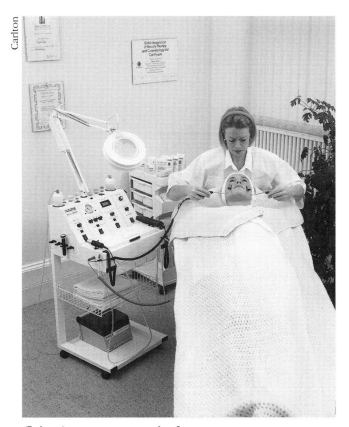

Galvanic treatment on the face

under the plinth cover for comfort), so that the client is well insulated and the current cannot escape to earth.

6 Do not apply the treatment over cuts, wounds or small breaks in the skin as these allow the current to enter the skin easily at this point, concentrating it and causing an unpleasant sensation with the risk of a burn. A petroleum jelly coating over the break can help to minimise this, but extra care must be taken.

7 Before treatment, ensure that the skin is thoroughly clean. Use appropriate cleansers and toners on the face and on the body.

8 During body work, the electrodes must be very firmly strapped in place to maintain good contact throughout the treatment. The sponge cloth (Spontex) covers should not be creased and should cover every bit of the electrodes and connections. Any bare area left in contact with the skin will cause a burn. Take care to also cover any crocodile clip connections.

9 Always make sure that the intensity controls are turned to zero at the start and again at the end of each treatment.

10 Make sure that the polarity of the electrode matches that specified by the manufacturers of the gels and solutions used, as these vary.

11 During the treatment, make sure that the hand-held electrodes are evenly covered with a good thickness of evenly damp Spontex. Any unevenness in dampness or thickness will concentrate the current.

12 Always turn the current up and down very slowly, watching the client's reactions all the time. On the face, the current should be increased slowly until the client feels a sensation, then reduced so that it is applied below the level of detection. On the body, it is wise not to exceed 4.25 milliamps. Anything above this can cause blisters to occur after the treatment has taken place. An erythema (slight redness) of the skin, especially under the negative electrode, is desirable. It is dangerous to increase the current after this point.

13 Do not apply the treatment for too long: 3–7 minutes are sufficient for facial work, depending on which gels or creams are being used; 25–30 minutes are sufficient for body work. Follow the treatment times recommended by the manufacturer of the gels or solutions used.

14 After treatment, cleanse the area again to remove any acids or alkalis formed by the treatment. Use cleansers for the face, warm water for the body. Most of these deposits will have been absorbed by the Spontex pads during a body treatment, and these pads and the securing straps must be thoroughly washed and

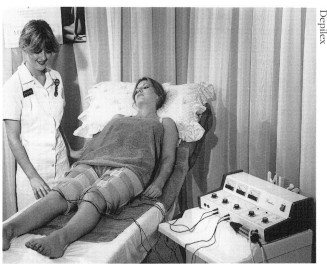

Galvanic treatment on the body

dried between each use, both for reasons of hygiene and to prevent their decay.

15 To complete the body treatment, apply unperfumed talcum powder to the area which has been treated. For the facial treatment, continue as instructed by the product manufacturers.

• • • • • • CONTRAINDICATIONS • • • • • •

– pacemakers or metal implants in the body, including copper contraceptive devices – these will concentrate the current and cause internal burning
– pregnancy
– high blood pressure
– heart conditions
– varicose veins
– skin infections
– any lack of skin sensitivity
– cuts, wounds or abrasions
– pustular conditions

If in doubt, e.g. with clients who have epilepsy or diabetes, obtain their doctor's permission before carrying out treatment.

Hand-held hair dryers

• • • • • • • • DANGERS • • • • • • • •

Burns, electric shock and scalp lesions.

• • • • • • • PRECAUTIONS • • • • • • •

1 Always choose a hand-held dryer with a good hair guard covering the air intake. Hair drawn into an uncovered vent can become tangled around the fans and, if this happens, hair is torn from the scalp very rapidly, often causing severe scalp damage. This precaution is especially important if the dryers are supplied for client use in beauty salons or health clubs. In these situations, purpose-built, wall-mounted models with flexible ducting leading to a hot-air nozzle are available. These are much safer for client use.

2 Remember to remove and clean the hair guard on hand-held dryers frequently. Failure to do this will result in the appliance over-heating, with the consequent danger of electric shock and burns to the user.

3 Do not use a temperature setting that is too high. This could result in scalp burns or

damaged hair. Purpose-built wall dryers usually operate at a pre-fixed warm setting and should be checked regularly to ensure that this is maintained at its correct level.

High frequency

• • • • • • • • • DANGERS • • • • • • • • •

Small burns and electric shock.

• • • • • • • • PRECAUTIONS • • • • • • •

1 Do not make sparks near the eyes or mouth.
2 Use a natural, not a synthetic, fabric between the electrode and the skin. If synthetic fabric is used, the sparks may cause it to melt and inflict nasty pinprick burns on the client.
3 Both the client and the therapist must remove all jewellery if an indirect application of high frequency is to be made, otherwise the metal will concentrate the current and cause a burn.

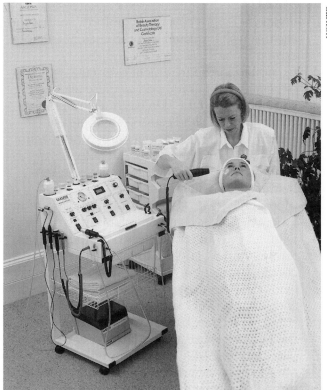

High-frequency treatment

Carlton

4 Do not use with any volatile substance capable of producing an inflammable vapour, e.g. preparations containing alcohol. The sparks from the electrode would cause flash ignition of any vapour created.

5 The electrode must be in contact with the client's skin before being turned on and after the machine is turned off.

6 Make sure that there is no metal or moisture in contact with the client during the treatment. This can cause a burn by concentrating the current in a limited area.

• • • • • • CONTRAINDICATIONS • • • • • •

– heart conditions
– epilepsy
– asthma
– excessive number of amalgam fillings in teeth

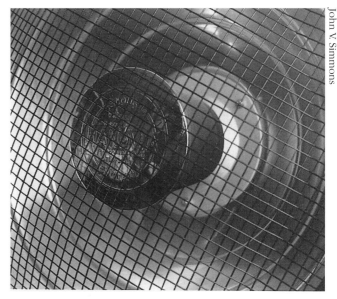

An infra-red generator

Infra-red heat

• • • • • • • • DANGERS • • • • • • • • •

Fire, burns, electric shock, eye damage, headaches and dizziness.

• • • • • • • PRECAUTIONS • • • • • • • •

1 Do not let the client touch or move the equipment.

2 Do not place the lamp directly over the client. Allow a distance of at least half a metre from the client, choosing a distance which is comfortable, warming and tolerable to the client.

3 Check that the client is able to feel hot and cold sensations.

4 Do not irradiate the area for too long and keep it uncovered so that the therapist can easily see the extent of any erythema. The therapist must not leave the client during treatment.

5 Tell the client to inform you if the lamp feels too hot.

6 Keep inflammable material well away from the lamp.

7 Protect the eyes of the client with goggles if the treatment is given near to the eyes.

8 Do not give infra-red treatment to a client who normally gets headaches in hot weather. Headaches are often linked to lack of perspiration during a treatment. Give the client water to drink to encourage perspiration.

9 Make sure that the lamp is switched off after the treatment is completed.

Laser treatments

• • • • • • • • DANGERS • • • • • • • • •

Retinal damage, electric shock, fire.

• • • • • • • PRECAUTIONS • • • • • • • •

1 Both the operator and the client should wear some form of suitable eye protection while the machine is in operation. On no account must anyone stare into or at a laser beam.

2 Class 2 lasers – those emitting visible radiation of a wavelength between 300 and 700 nanometres and having a maximum power output of 1 milliwatt – are the only lasers suitable for safe use in a beauty salon. Class 3 lasers are too highly powered.

3 Lasers should always be used in brightly lit conditions without reflective surfaces and away from inflammable targets.

4 The thyroid area should be avoided as it is not yet known what effects the beam could have on this gland.

• • • • • • CONTRAINDICATIONS • • • • • • •

- the presence of warts, moles and lumps which may become malignant if irradiated
- infectious and contagious skin conditions
- diabetes
- epilepsy
- heart pacemakers
- headaches

Manicure and pedicure

• • • • • • • • DANGERS • • • • • • • •

Scalds, minor cuts, allergies.

• • • • • • • PRECAUTIONS • • • • • • • •

1 To avoid transmission of infection, always wipe the client's hands with a proprietary antiseptic prior to treatment. Add an antiseptic soaking solution to the foot bath used in pedicures.
2 Never file nails too vigorously. The edge of a file makes a dangerous cutting implement when drawn rapidly against the nail wall.
3 Always take care when clipping cuticles. A minimum border of 1 mm must be left intact to allow the cuticle to do its job of preventing infection from getting into the nail area. Cuts in this area bleed profusely and are quite painful and prone to infection for a few days afterwards due to their exposed position. This also applies to injuries inflicted by a file.
4 Take care that cuticle clippers are always sharp. Torn cuticles can result from clipping with blunt implements.
5 Always test the temperature of the water in manicure and pedicure bowls before giving them to clients. Water which is too hot can damage the linkages in the nail plate and lead to flaking and peeling nails, as can the use of detergents in the soaking water. Non-detergent, moisturising solutions should be used for the soaking procedure.
6 Care must be taken when pushing back the cuticles. Over-enthusiastic work here can give rise to cross-ridging of the growing nail plate or paronychia (infection of the tissues surrounding the nail).

7 A rash around the client's face, neck or nails could be due to an allergy to the nail polish or products used.
8 Excessive use of strong, acetone-based nail polish removers can dehydrate and damage the surface of the nail. More gentle, non-acetone removers should be used no more than once a week.
9 Some nail plates dehydrate and become rough as a reaction to the polishes used. This reaction seems to occur most frequently with synthetic pearlised polishes. Try changing to matt polishes first, and if this does not work, change the make of polish used on the client.
10 When nail polish is peeled away, it takes some of the surface cells of the nail with it, weakening and thinning the nail plate. Always use nail polish removers.
11 Many manicure products are inflammable, e.g. polishes, removers and thinners. Do not smoke when near them.
12 The removal of hard skin from the feet using a credo blade is best left to a chiropodist. However, if it is undertaken in the salon, a new blade must be used for each client and disposed of in a sharps container. The blade holder must be sterilised between each use, along with metal and synthetic files, cuticle clippers, and any other small sterilisable equipment.

• • • • • • CONTRAINDICATIONS • • • • • •

- a nail which shows any signs of disease, inflammation, pus or pain, e.g. onychia (inflammation of the nail bed) – refer to a doctor
- psoriasis and eczema (inflammation of the skin)
- any fungal, bacterial or viral skin conditions, e.g. ringworm and athlete's foot (fungal), impetigo (bacterial), or common and flat warts (viral) – refer to a doctor
- any fungal, bacterial or viral infection of the nail, usually identified by a brown, green, black, yellow/grey or white discolouration, crumbling of the nail plate, or separation of the nail plate from the nail bed – refer to a doctor

It is also inadvisable to carry out any cuticle clipping, hard skin paring or harsh rasping on people with diabetes or poor peripheral blood circulation as their skin is both very slow to heal and prone to infection.

Massage

•••••••••DANGERS•••••••••

There are no real dangers associated with massage as long as the operator has undergone training in this field.

•••••••PRECAUTIONS•••••••

1 Make sure that the plinth is sturdy and safe.
2 Make sure that the client is kept adequately covered and warm, thus avoiding chills.
3 Towels and plinth covers must be changed and hygienically laundered for each client in order to avoid the spread of infection. A pre-massage shower for the client is also a good idea for the same reason.
4 Make sure that the floor covering around the plinth is non-slip.
5 Supervise the client while they are getting on and off the plinth, to ensure that they do not fall.

••••••CONTRAINDICATIONS••••••

Massage should not be carried out:

– over recent scars or operations – the scar tissue may part if the massage movement is too vigorous
– over varicose veins
– over areas of broken skin
– over excessive hairy areas, as skin irritation may develop
– where any skin disorders are present, e.g. eczema, or where any contagious condition is present
– below a swollen area, e.g. a sprain – massage should always be above and away from these areas.

Do not use tapotement over bony areas, and avoid abdominal massage in the 2–3 days before or during a menstrual period, during pregnancy, and where the client is suffering or has suffered a recent attack of gastro-enteritis.

If there is a severe medical condition, e.g. cancer, the written permission of the client's physician is needed before undertaking treatment.

Nail extensions and repairs

This section applies to acrylic, gel, fibreglass and stick-on full nails. See also page 113, nail extension injuries.

•••••••••DANGERS•••••••••

Damage to the nail surface and surroundings, allergy, fungal infections, inhalation of fumes, fragments of nail entering and piercing the eye.

•••••••PRECAUTIONS•••••••

1 Always work in a cool and well-ventilated area. The fumes from the nail liquid, sprays and glues used are strong and could cause headaches, respiratory disorders, dizziness or fainting if inhaled. Deck extractor fans are essential where strong chemicals are in use.
2 Do not file the surface of the natural nail prior to artificial nail application. This will weaken the nail plate, and may also damage the cuticle area. For this reason, extreme caution must also be taken when using an electric nail file to prepare the area for artificial nail infills or application.
3 Make sure that the area of work, the materials and equipment used, your hands and the client's hands and nails are cleansed by using proprietary antiseptic, disinfectant and sterilising agents both before and during the application of artificial nails. In this way the risk of fungal and other infections can be minimised.
4 Extreme caution must be taken during clipping back prior to infilling an acrylic nail. The acrylic nail can be very brittle (especially if the client has been using nail glue in between infill treatments) and the small pieces can fly off suddenly at great speed. Ideally, there should be a transparent screen placed between the nails being clipped and the eyes of both manicurist and client. Failing this, the manicurist and the client need to wear protective goggles during this procedure.
5 Clients with artificial nails must receive regular nail infill treatments, i.e., once every two weeks at the least. A manicure on the weeks in between should be strongly recommended (if not obligatory) so that a constant check can be kept on the condition of the nails. Clients with full plastic artificial nails must also be encouraged to have them checked weekly, and

replaced every two weeks. If the artificial nail lifts at the base, or a large regrowth gap is allowed to develop, there is a risk of damage to the natural nail underneath. A common injury is where the nail splits through to the nail bed. This can occur if the stiff artificial nail is caught or banged in a way which would cause a bend at the junction between the artificial and real nail.

TIP BOX

Lifting usually occurs because of poor product application or neglect. Every time an artificial nail lifts away from the natural nail surface it takes a layer of natural nail with it, thinning and damaging the natural nail plate.

6 Do not apply an artificial nail that is too long as this may result in damage (bruising, splitting, lifting, onycholysis) to the natural nail. Nails which are too long can also result in muscle wastage in the hands where clients are unable to use them properly. Aim for a maximum total of $1\frac{1}{2}$ times the length of the client's nail bed. First fittings, especially on very short nails, should be shorter than this.

A fibreglass extension

7 Avoid excessive use of nail glues as these can indirectly damage the nail plate, making it brittle, flaky and fragile.

8 Do not allow naked flames or smoking in the artificial nail application area as the solutions and nail products used are highly inflammable.

9 If allergies arise, they are usually, but not always, caused by the monomer component of the products used. There is no cure for an allergy. The offending product must not be used again.

•••••• CONTRAINDICATIONS ••••••

Do not apply false nails where:

– the nail plate is completely split through below the flesh line. Infection may already be present but not obvious. The false nail would seal the infection into the nail bed where it could cause a lot of damage

– the cuticles are badly split

– any hand or nail infection is present

– any of the usual contraindications to manicure exist (see page 66).

Non-surgical face and body lifting

These techniques use special weak micro-electric currents to stimulate the muscles, shortening and bringing them into tone. They improve blood circulation and lymphatic drainage.

•••••••• DANGERS •••••••••

Electric shock (see electrical equipment, page 26).

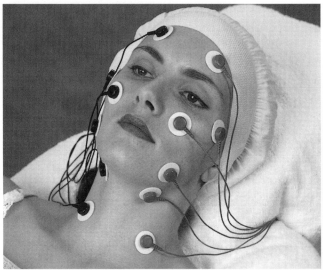

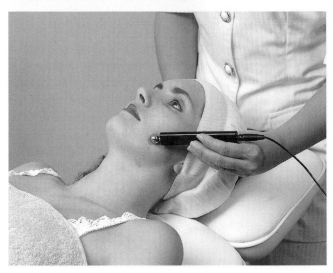
Non-surgical face lifting

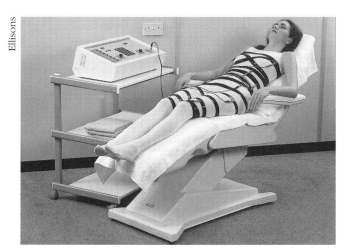

Body slimming

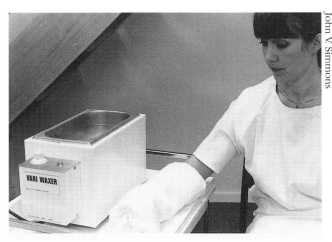

Paraffin waxing

• • • • • • • **PRECAUTIONS** • • • • • • • •

It is recommended that clients do not receive more than two sessions a week.

• • • • • • **CONTRAINDICATIONS** • • • • • •

– open cuts – cover with petroleum jelly
– varicose veins
– muscle disease
– pregnancy
– after childbirth, or any operation, until the doctor's permission has been given
– high blood pressure
– heart conditions
– epilepsy or diabetes
– pacemakers

If in doubt, seek medical advice and permission.

Paraffin waxing

• • • • • • • • **DANGERS** • • • • • • • • •

Scalds, fire.

• • • • • • • • **PRECAUTIONS** • • • • • • • •

1 Keep the wax well away from flames or direct heat. Paraffin wax is one of the most flammable substances known. Always use equipment which has been specifically designed for heating paraffin wax, as this eliminates fire risk and, to a certain extent, overheating.
2 For hygienic reasons, do not reuse wax which has been used for body treatments.

3 Do not reuse wax which has been used in conjunction with essential oils, as these remain in the wax and active.
4 When treating pain in muscles and joints, do not allow the wax temperature to exceed 43°C as these clients often have heightened sensitivity to heat. Always check the temperature of the wax on yourself before applying the wax to the client.
5 For facial treatments, do not allow the temperature of the wax to exceed 43–46°C.
6 For paraffin therapy treatments on the body, do not allow the temperature of the wax to exceed 53°C.

• • • • • • **CONTRAINDICATIONS** • • • • • •

– skin diseases
– cuts and abrasions
– warts
– moles
– pustules
– stings
– varicose veins and sensitive skin
– diabetes

Sauna and steam baths

• • • • • • • • **DANGERS** • • • • • • • • •

Scalds, burns, fainting, heat stroke and exhaustion with resulting collapse, falls, headaches, infection, fatigue.

•••••••PRECAUTIONS•••••••

1 Take the client's pulse rate and temperature before and after treatment. Check the feet for fungal infections. Disposable 'slippers' should be supplied.

2 Check equipment temperatures before use and at frequent intervals to guard against thermostat failure. Make sure the thermostat controls are out of reach of the client.

3 Make sure that there is an efficient guard around the heater or steam inlet.

4 Keep the client in view throughout the treatment.

5 Do not treat the client for too long. Different people need different lengths of time. The usual length of a sauna or steam room treatment is 20–30 minutes, with a shower or plunge included in the middle of this time. Individual steam baths are usually of shorter duration, around 15–20 minutes.

6 Do not overheat the client. The temperature range in the sauna should be 60–80°C. Take special care with new clients unused to the treatment. The lower benches have the lower temperature. A steam bath should have a temperature range of only 50–55°C.

7 Give the client clear instructions on correct usage of the equipment, and place a poster repeating these instructions in a prominent position.

8 Make sure that there is adequate resting space. A place should be provided for clients to cool down and have a drink before leaving the premises. Clients should rest for 30 minutes to one hour after the treatment.

9 Ensure that there is a good non-slip covering on the floor in and around the cubicle.

10 Make sure that dressing gowns and towels are only used once before being hygienically laundered. Disposable slippers should be used.

••••••CONTRAINDICATIONS••••••

– high or low blood pressure
– heart complaints
– breathing difficulties, e.g. asthma
– pregnancy

A sauna

A steam bath

Semi-permanent make-up (micropigmentation)

• • • • • • • DANGERS • • • • • • • •

Transmission of infection; increased risk of scarring and keloid formation on black skin.

• • • • • • • PRECAUTIONS • • • • • • •

1 Semi-permanent make-up, which places pigment in the epidermis and gradually fades over 1–3 years due to exfoliation, is not to be confused with a cosmetic tattoo which places the pigment permanently in the dermis. However, because the skin is being pierced with a needle and there is risk of infection and possible blood-to-blood contact, both treatments must be carried out under conditions of strict hygiene using disposable needles. Used needles must be disposed of safely in sharps containers (see sterilisation and disinfection procedures, page 46).
2 Surgical rubber gloves must be worn when treating a client.
3 Make-up must not be worn on the treated area until complete healing has taken place – approximately three days. Only the appropriate aftercare products must be used on the area.

Showers

• • • • • • • DANGERS • • • • • • • •

Falls, scalds.

• • • • • • • PRECAUTIONS • • • • • • •

1 Explain the use of the shower controls to each client before use.
2 Make sure that there is a good non-slip mat on the base of the shower cubicle.
3 Make sure that clients dry their feet before leaving the shower area.
4 Check the thermostatic control on the shower unit frequently.
5 If possible, fit the shower with a hand rail to hold. A shower seat could be installed for elderly clients if appropriate.

Sugaring

This section applies to the use of sugaring for hair removal.

• • • • • • • DANGERS • • • • • • • •

Removal of epidermal tissue, bruising.

• • • • • • • PRECAUTIONS • • • • • • •

1 Never reuse sugar on different clients as this could cause a spread of infection.
2 Due to the risk of blood spots, rubber gloves should always be worn by the therapist when carrying out hair-removal treatments.
3 Do not carry out a sugaring treatment immediately after a solarium treatment or heat treatment, as this makes the skin more susceptible to lifting.
4 Try not to carry out a sugaring treatment prior to or during a menstrual period. The skin is more sensitive at this time and may react unpredictably. The client's pain threshold is also lower at this time, making the treatment more unpleasant.
5 It is best to avoid the sensitive area below the eyebrows. Reactions, e.g. severe swelling and inflammation, are common and unpredictable, although often linked to the menstrual cycle.
6 If the client's skin starts lifting away during the treatment, the treatment must be postponed and first aid applied to the affected area (see page 117).
7 Take special care where the client is tanned or has just returned from a sunbathing holiday, as the outer epidermis will be loose and liable to tear away with the sugar.
8 Firmly stretch and support the skin in fleshy areas, e.g. the bikini line and underarm areas, otherwise bruising may occur.
9 Apply cold compresses to the bikini line, underarm and top lip areas immediately after the treatment to alleviate discomfort.
10 A proprietary antiseptic aftercare lotion should be used to avoid possible infection of the empty follicles and help soothe any skin irritation resulting from the treatment.

• • • • • CONTRAINDICATIONS • • • • • •

– varicose or broken veins
– skin complaints or infections
– broken skin

– recent scar tissue
– excessive ingrowing hairs from a previous treatment
– prior to or during a menstrual period

Ultrasound

Ultrasound equipment sends high-frequency ultrasound waves out in a straight line to penetrate the skin up to depths of approximately 7 cm. The sound waves set up micro-vibrations in the tissues, giving a micromassage to break down fatty and calcium deposits, stimulate the blood circulation and produce heat. In beauty therapy, ultrasound is mainly used for breaking down cellulite deposits and mobilising fatty tissues.

• • • • • • • • • DANGERS • • • • • • • • •

Deep and surface tissue and bone burns.

• • • • • • • • • PRECAUTIONS • • • • • • • •

1 Ultrasound does not travel through air, but through oils, liquids or matter. Therefore an oil, liquid or gel must be used to maintain good contact and conduction between the transmitting head and the body area being treated.
2 The ultrasound waves travel in a straight line and vibrate the tissues to give them a micromassage and build up heat within them. It is therefore important to keep the transmitting head moving all the time during a treatment to prevent heat build-up and subsequent deep or shallow tissue burns in any one area.

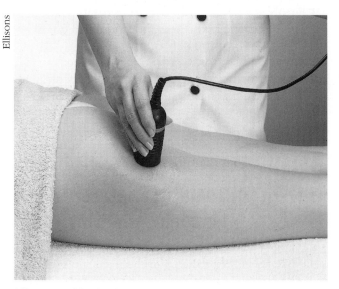

Ultrasound body therapy

Ellisons

3 The transmitting head must be applied to the body before the machine is switched on at the start of the treatment, and the machine must be switched off before the transmitting head is removed at the end of the treatment.
4 Equipment used in beauty salons to treat cellulite should have a power level of no more than 1–2 watts and not penetrate the skin to depths greater than 3 cm, i.e. not beyond the fatty tissue.
5 Treatments should be carried out no more than twice a week to ensure that the lymphatic system does not become overloaded with the products released during the micromassage.

• • • • • • CONTRAINDICATIONS • • • • • •

– acute inflammation
– acute rheumatism
– vascular problems, e.g. varicose veins or thrombosis
– circulation deficiencies
– blood clotting disorders
– neuralgia
– up to 8 months after deep X-ray therapy
– tumours
– pregnancy
– metal implants in the body
– pacemakers

Ultra-violet tanning therapy

• • • • • • • • • DANGERS • • • • • • • • •

Overdose, burns, eye exposure causing damage to the eye, conjunctivitis, skin sensitivity, headaches, excess ozone production, broken facial capillaries due to excessive exposure, allergies, heat exhaustion.

> **TIP BOX**
>
> An HSE leaflet, *Commercial Ultra-Violet Tanning Equipment* (INDG209), provides comprehensive information on long- and short-term health risks and safety precautions to be taken when using ultra-violet equipment. It is available free of charge. As every client must by law be aware of this information, it is a good idea to reproduce the contents of this leaflet and give them a copy. All HSE publications are available from HSE Books (address on page 122).

• • • • • • • PRECAUTIONS • • • • • • • •

1 Tanning equipment should be of sturdy construction. The frame and perspex should easily withstand the impact of a heavy, falling person.

2 Hydraulic lifting apparatus or ceiling-suspended apparatus should be substantial, safe and regularly checked.

3 Clients should not have access to the timing mechanisms and should not touch the bulbs or burners. They should, however, have ready and known access to an off switch and a source of help (see point 6).

4 Ventilation should be good, but without draughts.

5 When using apparatus which requires a client to turn over half way through the treatment period, do not simply leave the client alone with a timer – they may fall asleep. Either check at half time to ensure that they have turned over, or provide a timer which rings continuously until the client is disturbed and has to move in order to turn it off.

6 The client should be able to reach a 'panic' or help button in the cubicle in order to summon assistance if necessary. An emergency switch-off mechanism should also be convenient for the client to reach.

7 A trained operator should be within easy listening distance of the tanning cubicle at all times to cope with any eventualities which may

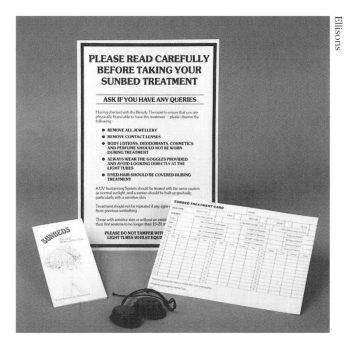

arise. However, the operator must not be subjected to the light from the equipment during client treatment.

8 If possible, disposable floor coverings should be used to prevent the spread of verrucae, and a clean headrest covering provided for each client.

9 A warning notice should be displayed prominently in the cubicle, stating clearly the hazards of the equipment and the correct procedure to be followed. This could include the following:

> **Do** wear the goggles provided.
> **Do** only allow half the full exposure time on sensitive areas, e.g. bust/bottom.
> **Do** inform staff if you are taking any drugs whatsoever – this includes HRT and the pill.
> **Do** drink more fluids to replace those lost by sweating.
> **Do** remove contact lenses before use.
> **Don't** drink alcohol before use.
> **Don't** use deodorants/colognes before going on the bed and remember that cosmetics screen rays from your face.

10 Use a proprietary equipment cleanser between clients. Antiseptics and disinfectants can often cause skin reactions in clients and may damage the equipment.

11 A client who has any cosmetics or deodorants on the body or face must shower thoroughly before the treatment, otherwise their skin could be sensitised by the products.

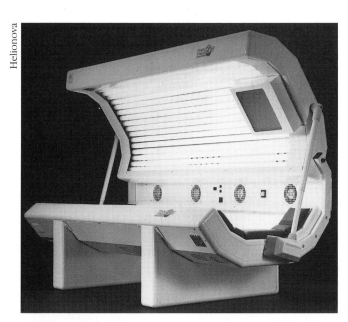

A UVA sunbed

12 The client must wear protective actinotherapy goggles during the treatment (sunglasses are not sufficient). The goggles must be disposable or cleaned between treatments using a suitable bactericide. Children must not be allowed in the cubicle while a treatment is being carried out.

13 Contact lenses must be removed before treatment or the lenses could concentrate the rays and cause damage to the eyes.

14 Warn clients who have returned from sunbathing holidays to cover any areas that have not been tanned for half the recommended exposure time – these areas will burn if exposed to the same amount of radiation as the tanned areas. If covering is worn during a treatment, the same items must be worn at each treatment to ensure that the same areas are exposed to the rays.

15 Any client who has burns from normal sunbathing must not be allowed to use tanning equipment until all signs of redness and burning have disappeared.

16 Do not give tanning treatment immediately after other treatments which raise the temperature of the skin, e.g. waxing, electrolysis, sauna or heavy massage, as these will sensitise the skin and a reaction could occur.

17 Any client suffering from itchiness after treatment must not be allowed back on the equipment until the itching has gone completely. After this, the treatment times must be reduced and then very gradually increased to allow the skin to become accustomed to the ultra-violet rays.

18 Clients must be encouraged to shower after the treatment if they have been perspiring, as a rash can develop if perspiration is allowed to dry on the body.

19 Drinks and a cooling-down area must be provided for the clients' use after treatment.

TIP BOX

The Government Health Guidelines stipulate that it is best not to exceed more than 20 tanning sessions a year.

Initial consultation

An initial consultation is vital to determine the client's skin type and suitability for the treatment. A record card should be filled in and the client questioned about their recent medical background (within the past two months). One side of the card should contain a client questionnaire, a list of instructions for the correct and safe use of the tanning equipment, and warnings as to the potential short- and long-term hazards of ultra-violet rays. Clients should be asked to read this carefully and then to sign it to show that they fully understand the risks and procedures associated with ultra-violet tanning treatments.

Clients should declare that they are not taking any medication or suffering from any stated contra-indications to use, and that they accept liability for any effects arising from disregarding the written instructions. If a client is suffering from any medical condition, receiving any medical treatment, or taking any drugs, they must be asked to obtain a letter from their doctor stating that it is safe for them to have ultra-violet treatment. This letter must be placed in the client's file and updated at six-monthly intervals, or at the start of each new course of treatment.

Equipment and treatment times

Old-type **solaria** emit a lot of ultra-violet rays in a very short time, and a large proportion of these rays are in the burning ultra-violet B category. The skin can be burned within a few minutes, hence the recommended times of use start at one minute.

High-pressure units emit a lot of ultra-violet rays in a very short time, with proportionally fewer ultra-violet B rays than solaria, but still sufficient to burn the skin in a short time. These units are placed behind filter glass to screen out some of the ultra-violet B rays. The recommended times of use start at around 4–5 minutes.

Tanning tubes emit fewer ultra-violet rays in a given time than either solaria burners or high-pressure units. Tanning tubes also emit the lowest proportion of ultra-violet B rays and so have the least risk of burning the skin. Their recommended times of use start at around 5–10 minutes, and a treatment can last considerably longer than this depending on the client's skin type and the make and model of the tube.

It is important to keep a record of how long tubes or burners have been in use. Some equipment comes with an in-built timer to add up the total running hours. Extra care must be taken with new equipment, tubes or burners, as during the first 100 hours of use they emit very high amounts of radiation and this can easily burn the client if the treatment is not strictly monitored. After this period, the radiation emission becomes less intense – although still effective for tanning purposes. To maintain maximum safety and effectiveness, follow the recommendations of your particular equipment manufacturer regarding hours of usage and suitable replacement tubes or burners.

TIP BOX

When tubes or burners are replaced, clients may fail to realise the difference in strength between the new and old equipment. A client may try to demand an exposure time which is far too long, and would be burned if you agreed. Explain the situation to the client to avoid any bad feeling.

It is important to set suitable and safe treatment times for each individual client according to skin colouring and condition. Client skin colouring can be determined by observing the eye and hair colour, and the colour of the inside of the upper arm. Initial and subsequent tanning sessions should be strictly timed according to this information. Skin colouring can fall into one of four categories:

- red heads and very fair colouring (highly sensitive skin – short sessions)
- medium to fair colouring (medium to sensitive skin)
- medium colouring
- dark olive and well-tanned skins (maximum sessions).

TIP BOX

Don't forget that a client with a tanned face and body may not have a tanned bottom!

There are so many different types, numbers and combinations of tubes and burners on the market that no general guideline for treatment times can be given. It is important to follow the guidelines laid down by the supplier of your equipment, both for treatment times and tube/burner renewal.

TIP BOX

Due to the wide variety of tanning equipment available, it is very important that tanning equipment is used with extreme caution and that the manufacturer's instructions for use are followed implicitly.

The sessions should be started at the minimum recommended time for the relevant skin type and increased for each treatment according to the tube/burner guidelines, up to the maximum advised. Only one such session should be allowed each day. If a client misses a session, the time should not be increased at the following session. If a client misses more than two visits, start the timing from the beginning again. A record of the client's exposure time at each treatment must be kept, and a note made of the client's reaction to each treatment.

TIP BOX

A client must not be allowed on to tanning equipment if they have been sunbathing the same day, and must be warned against sunbathing on the same day after a treatment.

• • • • • • CONTRAINDICATIONS • • • • • •

All types of ultra-violet tanning therapy should be avoided if the client:

- has arteriosclerosis; liver, heart and kidney disease; epilepsy; diabetes; tuberculosis; any infectious or contagious skin conditions; high and low blood pressure; or thyroid trouble
- is pregnant
- is using systemic photosensitisers, e.g. antibiotics, tranquillisers, blood pressure medication, contraceptives, thyroxine, alcohol, anti-diabetic drugs, diuretics or creams
- is wearing contact photosensitisers, e.g. cosmetics, hair preparations, after-shave lotions, colognes or deodorants
- has had previous radiation therapy, e.g. to treat cancer
- has unusual or numerous wart or mole-like growths on the skin which could be potentially cancerous

– has a large number of freckles and/or red hair
– has fair, sensitive skin which burns easily or tans slowly or poorly
– is under 16 years of age
– has a history of sunburn during childhood
– has a medical condition which is worsened by sunlight
– has a personal or family history of skin cancer.

Although not all antibiotics, tranquillisers and diuretics are systemic photosensitisers, many are and it is beyond the scope of a beauty therapist to determine which are safe and which are not. This decision must rest with a medically qualified person. If in doubt, obtain permission from the client's doctor before undertaking treatment.

Vacuum suction

• • • • • • • • DANGERS • • • • • • • •

Bruising, damage of tissues, spread of infection.

• • • • • • • PRECAUTIONS • • • • • • •

1 Make sure you use sufficient lubricant, of a non-absorptive type, e.g. liquid paraffin.
2 Always test the pressure of the equipment on yourself before using it on the client. Do not use too strong a pressure. You should be able to feel a definite suction pressure and the flesh should be raised up into the cup. The treatment should not be painful.
3 Make sure you select the correct applicator and size for the area to be worked upon.
4 Break the seal between cup and skin with the finger before trying to remove the cup from the body, otherwise the treatment will be painful for the client and may result in bruising.
5 Always sterilise the applicators after treatments.

• • • • • CONTRAINDICATIONS • • • • • •

– varicose veins
– broken capillaries, cuts or abrasions
– skin infections or complaints
– recent scars
– bony areas
– pregnancy

Vacuum suction should not be used on the abdomen shortly before and during menstruation.

Vibration equipment

• • • • • • • • DANGERS • • • • • • • •

Bruising, tissue damage, spread of infection.

• • • • • • • PRECAUTIONS • • • • • • •

1 Make sure that the applicators are securely attached to the machine and that the correct head has been chosen for the treatment.
2 Sterilise the applicators after each use.

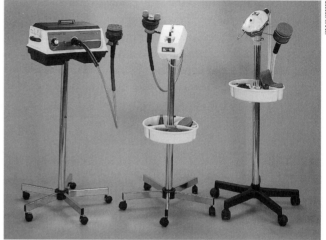

Ellisons

Vibration equipment

• • • • • CONTRAINDICATIONS • • • • • •

– bony areas
– broken veins
– varicose veins
– broken skin
– skin infections
– recent scars
– pregnancy

Do not use heavy applicators on the abdomen, and avoid this area shortly before or during the first 2–3 days of menstruation.

Waxing

This section applies to the use of organic and hot wax for hair removal.

• • • • • • • • DANGERS • • • • • • • •

Scalds, removal of epidermal tissue, bruising, fire, ingrowing hairs.

• • • • • • • PRECAUTIONS • • • • • • • •

General

1 Do not allow naked flames near waxing equipment as most wax preparations are inflammable.

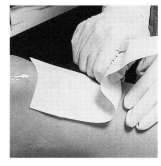

Waxing

2 Always test the heat of the wax before applying it to the client. Even with warm organic waxes, the thermostat could easily break on the heater and cause the wax to overheat.

3 Do not carry out a wax treatment immediately after a solarium treatment or heat treatment, as this makes the skin more susceptible to lifting.

4 Try not to carry out a wax treatment prior to or during a menstrual period. The skin is more sensitive at this time and may react unpredictably. The client's pain threshold is also lower at this time, making the treatment more unpleasant.

5 It is best to avoid the sensitive area below the eyebrows. Reactions, e.g. severe swelling and inflammation, are common and unpredictable, although often linked to the menstrual cycle.

6 If the client's skin starts lifting away during the treatment, then the treatment must be postponed and first aid applied to the affected area (see page 117).

7 Take special care where the client is tanned or has just returned from a sunbathing holiday, as the outer epidermis will be loose and liable to tear away with the wax.

8 Firmly stretch and support the skin in fleshy areas, e.g. the bikini line and underarm areas, otherwise bruising may occur.

9 Apply cold compresses to the bikini line, underarm and top lip areas immediately after the treatment to alleviate discomfort.

10 Use a proprietary antiseptic aftercare lotion to avoid possible infection of the empty follicles and help soothe any skin irritation resulting from the treatment.

11 Due to the risk of blood spots, rubber gloves should always be worn by the therapist when carrying out hair removal treatments.

12 Thorough moisturising after waxing can help to avoid the problem of ingrowing hairs. The client should be encouraged to buy and use one of the special aftercare moisturisers available for this purpose. (See also first aid, page 110.)

Organic waxing

1 Do not allow too much wax to build up on the muslin strip during use, as this can cause skin lifting during the removal process.

2 Keep your angle of pull on the muslin strip horizontal to the skin's surface, otherwise the hairs will tend to break off at the skin surface and bruising may occur in fleshy areas.

3 If you are using a wax which requires the area to be dusted with talcum powder prior to application, take care that talcum powder residue does not build up in the wax heater – this can cause alterations in the wax which may lead to surface burning of the client's skin upon application.

Hot waxing

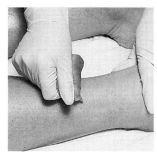

Hot waxing

1 Do not allow the wax to cool completely and thus become brittle on the client's skin before its removal. This would make the treatment both ineffective (hairs will tend to break off at the skin's surface) and very painful for the client.

2 Apply your hand to the depilated area firmly or with a gentle rubbing motion immediately after removal of the wax. This will relieve the stinging sensation felt by the client. This procedure is not possible with warm wax due to the sticky nature of the wax.

• • • • • • CONTRAINDICATIONS • • • • • •

– varicose or broken veins
– skin complaints or infections
– broken skin
– recent scar tissue
– excessive ingrowing hairs from a previous treatment
– prior to or during a menstrual period

If in doubt, obtain permission from the client's doctor before carrying out treatment.

Safety in the hairdressing salon

Accelerators

This section refers to radiated-light, dry-heat and infra-red accelerators.

• • • • • • • • DANGERS • • • • • • • • •

Burns, electric shock, damage to the eyes, damage to the hair due to dryness.

• • • • • • • • PRECAUTIONS • • • • • • • •

1 Ensure that the stand is firm and the equipment is not in a position where either the client or a member of the staff can knock it over, or trip over its cable.

An accelerator

2 Ensure that the equipment is evenly placed over and around the head so that the heat is evenly distributed over the hair, thus avoiding hot spots.

3 Ensure that the equipment is placed over the top and back of the head so that the bulbs or heat source are not pointing into or near the eyes – they could be damaged by the infra-red rays released.

4 Infra-red heat is very drying. Make sure that all the hair is well covered with the treatment product, e.g. conditioning cream, before using the equipment, as exposed hair could be damaged.

5 Accelerators are used to accelerate the absorption of conditioners or the speed of chemical reactions. Different types of accelerators work at different speeds; infra-red types are very efficient. Care must be taken to monitor the treatment being given so that over-processing and damage do not occur.

TIP BOX

The most recent models of infra-red equipment incorporate a moving heat source and fans to avoid the occurrence of 'hot spots'.

6 Stay within sight of your clients during treatment so that they can contact you quickly if they experience any difficulties, and so that you can check they are all right.

Aerosols

Hairdressers use many types of aerosol, from hairspray to mousses and foams.

• • • • • • • • DANGERS • • • • • • • • •

Explosion, fire, inhalation, damage to eyes or clothing.

• • • • • • • • PRECAUTIONS • • • • • • • •

1 Use aerosols only in well-ventilated areas to avoid build-up of fumes.

2 Do not inhale the sprays.

3 Do not spray into or near the eyes.

TIP BOX

A face shield can be used to protect the client's eyes and help them avoid excessive inhalation.

4 Do not use aerosols near open flames of any kind, heat lamps or dryers which are in use. Do not allow smoking anywhere nearby – the

propellants are highly inflammable and can allow flashback into the can with subsequent explosion.

5   Do not pierce or burn the aerosol containers, full or empty. Take care when using scissors around aerosols.

6   Keep all aerosols at room temperature or cooler, and do not place them in the sun. Do not use them in window displays or place them near boilers, heaters, radiators or hot-water cylinders.

7   Aerosols will explode in a fire. As such, they should be kept in a storage cupboard which will be resistant to fire for around 30 minutes. If there is a fire, the fire brigade must be notified of their presence and whereabouts as soon as they arrive.

8   Care should be taken to protect the clothing and skin of both the client and hairdresser when applying coloured aerosols or mousses.

Black hair

• • • • • • • DANGERS • • • • • • • •

Disguised sensitivity, keloid formation (lumps of skin tissue forming at the site of wounds), loss of pigmentation, extra sensitivity, hair breakage and damage.

• • • • • • PRECAUTIONS • • • • • • •

1   Take extra care when applying cosmetics or hair preparations of any kind to black hair and skin. Black skins have a tendency to be more sensitive and prone to allergies than white skins, and any reactions which do occur cannot be seen easily or quickly due to the masking effect of the coloured skin.

2   Always take extra care and carry out a skin test before using bleaching preparations on black skins. Unwanted side-effects can include permanently decolourised patches. Use plenty of barrier cream on any areas of skin with which chemicals, e.g. bleach, might come into contact, e.g. the hairline, ears and forehead areas.

3   Black Afro-Caribbean hair is weaker than European and Asian hair and this should be taken into account when performing any hair treatments, e.g. chemical treatments, combing, plaiting, beading, and adding hair extensions.

Clippers – electrical and mechanical

• • • • • • • • DANGERS • • • • • • • •

Electric shock, small cuts and infections from these, pulling hair out of the scalp.

• • • • • • • PRECAUTIONS • • • • • • •

Clippers

1   Ensure that you hold the clippers at the correct angle in relation to the skin, otherwise small cuts could occur.

2   Keep the wire well out of the way during use.

3   Make sure that the equipment is always kept clean, sharp and oiled so that the blades slide easily over one another. Failure to do this will result in the hair being pulled out instead of being cut by the blades, causing discomfort and annoyance to the client.

> **TIP BOX**
>
> **Doublecheck the positioning of the blades before starting. The top movable blade must not protrude beyond the bottom fixed blade or the skin will be cut.**

> **TIP BOX**
>
> **Disinfectant oils can be obtained with which to lubricate the clippers.**

4   Always use a new disposable blade for each client and dispose of it safely (see sterilisation and disinfection procedures, page 47).

TIP BOX

TIP BOX

Clipper heads must be removable to allow for cleaning between clients. Thorough cleaning and degreasing must be carried out before sterilisation in order for the procedure to be effective.

5 Extra care must be taken when using electric clippers on wet hair due to the risk of electric shock.

Clothing and gowning up

THE HAIRDRESSER

I A protective overall, offering good coverage, must be worn to protect the hairdresser from spillage of any harmful liquids.

2 Choice of shoes is important. As well as being comfortable, they should be almost flat and have non-slip soles to help prevent falls in the salon. Lace-ups are not recommended as these can lead to falls if the laces are not correctly tied. The shoes must protect the feet against spillage of hot liquids or chemicals, and against the entrance of hairs. A common problem for hairdressers is the entrance of cut hair into the skin via the pores or the area surrounding the toenails. Such hairs will cause infection and/or pain if not removed. Sandals should definitely be avoided. A suitable choice of shoes, with a small heel and sufficient arch support, will help to maintain or correct the posture, and help to avoid fatigue, tired legs and varicose veins.

3 Scissors, razors and knives must be kept in a sterile cabinet when not in use, not loose in pockets. As well as maintaining sterility, this will avoid the possibility of accidental cuts.

4 Rubber gloves must be worn when mixing and applying bleaches, permanent and semi-permanent colours, and when winding and redamping permanent waves.

Rubber gloves

These should be either disposable, or washed after use, then dried and sprinkled with talcum powder ready for their next use.

5 A separate apron must be worn for the above tasks and wiped clean (plastic) or washed (fabric) after every use to avoid residues of the products used being transferred elsewhere, e.g. to unprotected hands.

6 Protective eyeglasses must be worn when mixing any chemicals which could cause harm if they were to splash into the eye, e.g. bleaches, colours and perming solutions.

THE CLIENT

Clients must be adequately covered to protect them and their clothes from spillage or seepage of hot and cold liquids or chemicals.

For bleaching and colouring

I A light-coloured towel is placed around the client's neck and tucked firmly into the collar of any clothing to protect it from any seepage of the bleach.

Gowning up

2 A standard, back or front fastening, light-coloured hairdressing gown is then placed around the client's shoulders, with no opening showing.

3 A front-fastening, large waterproof cape is placed over the gown. This will also hang over the client's chair and completely protect them both.

4 A standard absorbent hairdressing towel is then draped around the client's neck and shoulders and tucked well in as a protection during the application of the bleach.

5 A barrier cream is applied to the client's forehead before any application of bleach or colour.

Note: gowning up for colour treatments involves the same procedure, except dark-coloured towels and a black gown should be used instead of light-coloured ones.

For perming

1 A standard hairdressing gown is placed around the client's shoulders.

2 A front-fastening waterproof cape is then placed over the gown.

3 A standard absorbent hairdressing towel is draped around the client's neck and shoulders and tucked well in to absorb any splashes of liquid. This particular towel is constantly checked, and changed if damp, during the whole of the perming process, i.e. after 'dabbing up' or rinsing. This is to avoid contamination between the perming solution and the neutraliser, and also to prevent any allergic reaction from occurring in the client's neck area.

4 A strip of cottonwool must be placed securely around the hairline before the perm solution is applied, and renewed before the application of the neutraliser. This is to prevent drips from entering the client's eyes.

> **TIP BOX**
>
> Check that the cottonwool around the hairline does not become soaked with perm solution or neutraliser. If it does, it must be changed or it will react with the skin.

5 A barrier cream should also be used to protect the forehead and all around the hairline, including behind the ears. Take care not to get the cream on the hair itself.

For shampooing

1 A standard hairdressing gown is placed around the client's shoulders.

2 A standard absorbent hairdressing towel is draped around the client's neck and shoulders and tucked well in to absorb any splashes of liquid.

3 If a front wash basin is used, a second absorbent towel should be given to the client to dry their face and prevent soapy water from entering the eyes during the shampooing process.

Note: this third stage also applies to shampooing and rinsing during the perming, colouring and bleaching processes.

Curling tongs, crimping irons, heated rollers and hot combs

• • • • • • • • DANGERS • • • • • • • •

Burns, electric shock, hair damage.

• • • • • • • PRECAUTIONS • • • • • • • •

1 Do not place this type of equipment up against the scalp, as it could burn the skin.

BaByliss

Heated curling brushes

Heated rollers

2 Exercise caution when timing the use of this type of equipment. If the treatment time is too long, the hair could be damaged.

3 Excessive use of this type of equipment can dry out and damage the hair. Again, caution must be exercised.

4 Due to the possible dangers of electrocution, extra care must be taken when using this type of equipment on wet hair.

TIP BOX

See page 26, electrical equipment, for general safety points regarding the use of all electrical items, and maintenance of equipment, plugs and wiring.

Hair dryers

• • • • • • • DANGERS • • • • • • • •

Burns, electric shock and scalp lesions.

• • • • • • PRECAUTIONS • • • • • • •

Hand-held dryers

I Always choose a hand-held dryer with a good hair guard covering the air intake. Hair drawn into an uncovered vent can become tangled around the fans and, if this happens, hair is torn from

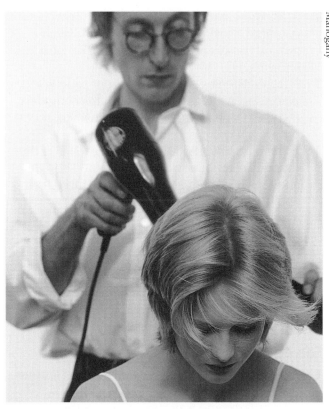

Using a hand-held hair dryer

the scalp very rapidly, often causing severe scalp damage. This precaution is especially important if the dryers are supplied for client use in beauty salons or health clubs. In these situations, purpose-built, wall-mounted models with flexible ducting leading to a hot-air nozzle are available. These are much safer for client use.

2 Remember to remove and clean the hair guard on hand-held dryers frequently. Failure to do so will result in the appliance over-heating, with the consequent danger of electric shock and burns to the operator.

3 Do not hold the dryer too near the client's hair or scalp, or use a temperature setting that is too high. This could result in scalp burns or damaged hair.

Fixed dryers

I If possible, try to check that the client's skin sensitivity is normal. If it is not, the client may burn under the dryer without realising it. This is a particular danger with elderly clients who may suffer from a loss of sensitivity as a result of ageing.

2 Check that the client knows where the thermostat controls are and how to adjust them.

3 Always stay within sight of your clients during a drying process so that they can contact you quickly if they experience any difficulties, and so that you can watch to see that they are all right.

4 If using metal rollers, place a strip of cottonwool under those around the hairline to prevent them from burning the forehead when they get hot.

A fixed dryer

Infra-red dryers

1 Ensure that the stand is substantial and firm and that it is positioned so that staff can walk around it without fear of knocking it over, and that the client cannot inadvertently knock it over. It is a good idea to set aside an area in which this apparatus can be used where these dangers are at a minimum.

2 When in use, do not allow any of the lamps to be closer than 20–25 cm from the client's hair. Make sure that the lamps are pointing at the hair from the back so that the infra-red rays do not shine into and harm the eyes of the client.

3 Always stay within sight of the client. Check regularly to ensure that the drying is even and that there is no risk of burning. The most recent infra-red dryers incorporate moving heat sources and fans to help overcome this problem.

4 In view of the 'dryness' of the infra-red heat, it is wise to avoid this method of drying on bleached or tinted hair as its use could lead to breakage of the hair.

Hair treatments – chemical

This section looks at bleaching, colouring and tinting, permanent waving, decolouring (colour stripping or reducing), recolouring and straightening. See also the section on hydrogen peroxide, page 90.

• • • • • • • • • DANGERS • • • • • • • • • •

Chemical burns and/or allergic reactions; splashing or running into and irritating or damaging the eyes; undesirable colour change in the hair; splitting and breakage of the hair; loss of condition of the hair.

• • • • • • • • PRECAUTIONS • • • • • • • •

General

1 Always administer a skin test 48 hours in advance of any proposed treatment to ensure the client is not allergic to the materials that are going to be used. Keep a record of this test on the client's record card along with other applicable details, e.g. other chemicals which have been used or treatments which the client has undergone in the past, especially those they have reacted against (see skin testing, page 44).

2 Be aware that allergy dermatitis, e.g. itching, red spots, vesicles, redness or oedema (fluid collection) can appear from a few to 48 hours after treatment. If it arises, it should be treated straight away (see page 97).

> **TIP BOX**
>
> **Black, Afro-Caribbean hair is one of the weakest types of hair, being very susceptible to breakage and splitting. Extra caution should be taken when performing chemical treatments on this type of hair.**

3 Do not use solutions which are unnecessarily strong. Always read the manufacturers' instructions and the relevant COSHH data sheets before using products. Take extra care with new products or products in new packaging as the instructions for use may have changed.

4 Keep all products well away from the client's eyes. The use of cottonwool strips around the

> **TIP BOX**
>
> **If there is any risk of chemicals splashing into the hairdresser's eyes, e.g. while mixing or applying products, protective glasses must be worn.**

margins of the hairline wherever possible helps to prevent drips from running into the eyes.

5 The use of a barrier cream on the client's forehead and all around the hairline will help to prevent allergy reactions and possible chemical burns in this area.

6 If the client has been swimming in chlorinated water prior to an appointment, care must be taken to ensure that no remnants of chlorine remain on the hair as this could have an adverse effect on the treatment or cause a sensitisation reaction. Special chlorine neutralising shampoos are available for this purpose.

TIP BOX

Check if your client has used any hair products containing metallic salts, e.g. metallic lacquer, in the month before treatment. Make sure that these salts are removed by shampooing thoroughly before treatment commences. To be completely sure the salts have been removed, take a cutting of hair and test the product you intend to use on this sample before undertaking the treatment on the hair.

7 At the end of a chemical treatment, always rinse thoroughly to avoid traces of the products used being left on the hair where they could continue working and/or cause sensitisation or allergy reactions. Many products include their own shampoo to use after the treatment, or have shampoo included in the product, as in colouring products, to ensure complete removal of the product used. It is also important to use a conditioner at the end of a treatment in order to leave the hair shaft in as good a condition as possible. The shampoos and conditioners used will vary depending on which product has been used on the hair.

8 Never carry out a perm on a client at the same time as a permanent colour or bleaching treatment. It is advisable to leave a minimum period of 48 hours, and preferably a week during which an additional shampoo has been carried out, between the two treatments. The scalp is softened and sensitised from the first product application, and is therefore more susceptible to

allergic reaction or chemical burn if another product is applied before it has had a chance to recover. This softening also applies to the hair shaft, making it more susceptible to damage.

TIP BOX

If chemical treatments were placed on a scale of severity (and difficulty) where 1 was the strongest and most potentially damaging treatment, it would look something like this:

1 **decolouring or colour stripping**
2 **bleaching dark hair to light**
3 **straightening naturally curly hair**
4 **bleached tips**
5 **straightening or loosening over-curled permed hair**
6 **permanent waving**
7 **colour lifting using a lightening colour**
8 **permanent colouring (e.g. covering grey hairs)**
9 **semi-permanent colours.**

Treatments 1–4 are the harshest and should only be carried out by well-qualified and experienced hairdressers. Such hairdressers will be able to judge if, when and how these treatments should be applied to the various types of hair, and also how long should be left between different treatments.

9 If the hairdresser chooses to carry out a treatment on the insistence of a client, knowing full well that the treatment is inadvisable and could have adverse effects on the client or their hair, the hairdresser will still be held liable in the eyes of the law if anything goes wrong, even if they are acting with the client's written permission. The hairdresser should have the best interests of the client in mind at all times and must refuse to do the treatment if, in their professional view, it is unsuitable for the client or their hair.

10 Every hairdresser is exposed to possible allergy reactions through the constant handling of the materials involved in these treatments. Sensitisation can occur even after years of constant contact with the products. In fact, it is often due to this constant contact that the

sensitisation develops. It is essential, therefore, that the hairdresser always wears rubber gloves or effective barrier products when working with chemicals, e.g. during the application of bleaches, straighteners or colourants, and during perm winding and neutralising.

Bleaching

TIP BOX

Any metal products which have to be used around chemicals, e.g. pin-tailed combs and sectioning clips, *must* be made of non-reactive stainless steel. If ferrous metals were to come into contact with both the hair and perm solutions, the iron salts in the metal would react with the perm solution to turn light-coloured hair pink. This can sometimes happen if a hairdresser doing a perm touches a ferrous metal, e.g. a handle on a trolley, and then touches the hair being permed. Chrome-plated products are not a satisfactory solution to this problem because the chrome wears away to reveal the ferrous metal underneath.

Bleaching

1 It is best not to shampoo the hair prior to bleaching, as the natural sebaceous coating of the scalp (sebum) forms a barrier between the chemicals to be used and the scalp. This barrier helps to protect the scalp against irritation due to contact with the chemicals used. However, an initial check must be made to ensure that the client does not have any lacquer or an excessive amount of dirt or grease on their hair as this would inhibit the action of the bleach. If there is any lacquer present, use a lacquer-removing shampoo and dry the hair completely prior to the treatment. Excessive dirt or grease can be removed with a neutral shampoo and the hair dried prior to treatment. Drying the hair is important so that the chemicals used will not be diluted by any moisture remaining on the hair.

2 Occasionally, clients use metallic lacquers on their hair. The metal salts in these lacquers penetrate the hair shaft and will need 4–5 shampoos to eliminate them from the hair completely. This is extremely important as a

---

TIP BOX

All-in-one shampoos tend to leave a residue on the hair shaft which can prevent hair treatments from being fully effective. Either get the client to use a normal shampoo for 3–4 washes before the proposed special treatment, or use a shampoo in the salon which will remove any residue on the hair.

TIP BOX

When bleaching root growth, hair conditioner can be put on the already bleached hair to protect and condition it during the treatment.

---

combination of the metal salts from the lacquer and a bleaching solution will cause a chemical reaction which will dissolve the hair (see also the tip box, page 84). It is not advisable to use a

L'Oréal

bleaching agent on the hair if a metallic lacquer has been used within the previous five shampoos.

TIP BOX

Always use non-metallic utensils and bowls when using hydrogen peroxide as metals will speed the decomposition of the product (see also hydrogen peroxide, page 90).

3 When mixing powder bleaches, ensure that you do so in a well-ventilated room as the fumes given off by the mixture are highly toxic. Wear a mask during this procedure to prevent inhalation of the fumes. Always follow the manufacturer's instructions carefully – powder strengths can vary as well as peroxide.

TIP BOX

Powder bleach is an oxidant. As such, it can spontaneously set on fire if allowed to stay in contact with inflammable materials such as paper or wood. Therefore, it is important to clean up spilled bleach powder immediately.

4 When, bleaching hair, do not use more than 12% (40 volume) peroxide – 9% (30 volume) is preferable and safer – as a stronger peroxide in combination with the bleaching powder can cause lesions of the scalp. Note: up to 18% (60 volume) can be used in conjunction with colours (see below), but care must be taken with bleach as the combination of bleaching powder and peroxide produces a fiercer and more severe effect.

5 Bearing in mind the guidelines in point 4, it is better to use a strong volume of peroxide for a short time rather than a weak volume for a long time. This is less damaging to the hair shaft and will provoke fewer allergy reactions in clients. The difficulty, however, is that the strength of the bleach to be used is limited by its irritating action on the scalp. Remember, no more than 12% (40 volume) peroxide should ever be used in conjunction with a bleach.

TIP BOX

Because the bleach does not come into contact with the scalp during the streaking/tipping process, up to 18% (60 volume) peroxide can be used during this treatment on resistant, e.g. red pigmented, hair. However, great care must be exercised!

6 Apply bleaching agent to the scalp area last of all on a full-head bleach, as the heat from the head will speed up the reaction time in this area. Start the application at the ends of the hair, progress to the middle length, and finish at the roots – except when the hair is long where the increased porosity at the ends of the hair will dictate application to the mid length first, then the ends, then the roots.

7 It is advisable to complete the treatment by using a shampoo and conditioner which will complement the brand of bleaching agent selected. The conditioner is particularly important as it is used to:

- counteract the decomposing effect that the peroxide has on the hair
- prevent creeping oxidisation, i.e. the bleached hair becoming lighter after the treatment is over due to bleach being left within the hair shaft, by containing an anti-oxidant to neutralise the bleach residue
- leave the hair in good condition.

TIP BOX

If anything goes wrong during or after carrying out a treatment, remember to notify the salon's insurance company straight away.

Colouring and tinting

1 It must be recognised that the higher volume peroxides are very dangerous chemicals. Inexperienced hairdressers should avoid using concentrations above 6–9% (20–30 volume) altogether. However, many of today's advanced colouring techniques do demand the use of up to 18% (60 volume) peroxide. In these

Regrowth tinting

circumstances, the amount of care required cannot be stressed too much and these treatments are best left to an experienced person, i.e. a colouring specialist, who knows the techniques, reactions and range of additives available to help minimise the decomposing effects which peroxide has on the hair. Under no circumstances should a concentration of peroxide greater than 18% (60 volume) be used on the hair, as anything stronger can cause lesions of the scalp.

2   After the treatment, shampoo with a neutral or slightly acid non-detergent shampoo (most manufacturers supply one to complement the colour or tint used) both to stop the reaction completely and also to prevent colour from being stripped out of the hair. This type of shampoo should also be used in subsequent washes, as a detergent type will slowly strip the hair of the colour you have just added.

3   Use a conditioner which will stop the decomposing action of the peroxide and leave the hair in good condition. Most manufacturers supply one to complement the colour or tint that has been used.

4   As with bleaching, it is best not to shampoo the hair prior to colouring or tinting, as the natural sebaceous coating of the scalp (sebum) forms a barrier between the chemicals used and the scalp (see also page 85).

5   Do not apply a colouring agent to hair on which metallic lacquer has been used within the previous five shampoos. This can result in a green cast developing on light-coloured hair due to the combination of the metal salts with the colouring agent (see also page 85).

TIP BOX

If a treatment results in the client's scalp breaking, swelling, blistering or becoming painful, send the client to the doctor immediately after making sure that all product has been rinsed from the hair and scalp.

Decolouring

1   Decolouring is one of the most potentially damaging jobs to be carried out in the hairdressing salon and requires a high level of skill and knowledge on the part of the operator. It must only be carried out by staff experienced in this type of work, and the manufacturer's instructions must be strictly followed.

2   Do not attempt to perm decoloured hair for at least a week after decolouring. Some hairdressers will not perm for at least a month after such a strong treatment, or not at all until the damaged hair has grown out. Professional judgement must be applied.

TIP BOX

Recolouring after decolouring is dependent on the decolourant used, so the manufacturer's instructions, helplines or advisory services must be referred to. Some manufacturers recommend immediate recolouring, but most advise that the hair should not be chemically processed again for some time after decolouring.

3 Do not use hydrogen peroxide in an attempt to remove compound henna or other vegetable or mineral (metallic) dyes. They are incompatible. Special colour reducers must be used to remove these dyes.

Recolouring

Red or warm shades must be applied to the hair before the final shade is applied, otherwise the hair can fade, become patchy, or even develop a greenish cast.

Permanent waving

1 Make sure the client's hair is shampooed before the treatment in order to eliminate all greasy substances and waste products clinging to it which might otherwise hinder or slow down the perming process.

> **TIP BOX**
>
> Henna coats the hair shaft in a way similar to an all-in-one shampoo/conditioner (see page 85). However, whereas all-in-one products shampoo out after a few washes, henna does not, and therefore makes the perming of henna-coloured hair extremely difficult, if not impossible in some cases. Always test the hair with both perm and neutraliser before attempting to perm hair coloured with henna.

2 Permanent waving solutions are, on the whole, alkaline substances of varying strengths. As such, if an acidic shampoo were used prior to the perming treatment, it would cause a reaction with the perm solution which would lengthen the development time to varying degrees. Acidic shampoos should therefore be avoided before a perm. Most companies now produce a neutral pre-perming shampoo, formulated to complement their own permanent waving solution, which will not interfere with its effects. It is advisable to use these to obtain the best results. If they are not available, use a shampoo with a pH as near to neutral as possible, as this will interfere least with the effects of the perming solution. Do not use specially formulated shampoos, e.g. lemon, beer, anti-dandruff or medicated shampoos, before perming as these can also alter the effects of the perming solution.

3 Do not rub the scalp too hard during shampooing as this could sensitise it to the permanent waving solution.

> **TIP BOX**
>
> Any metal tools used during perming, e.g. pin-tailed combs and clips, must be made of non-reactive stainless steel.

4 Care must be taken to wind the hair evenly on the permanent waving curlers, and to ensure that the hair is not too tight or too loose. An even tension is essential to give an even result which reproduces the shape of the curlers.

5 It is especially important not to wind too tightly or allow the hair to dry out during a heat-assisted perming process. If the hair is too tight the sudden application of heat could cause it to break off at the roots as the hair dries out and therefore contracts upon heating. If the heat source is too hot, this would also lead to breakage of the hair at the roots. For this reason, it is very important to check that the thermostat on the heat source is working properly prior to each treatment.

6 Be careful not to process the perm for too long – over-processing will harm the shaft of the hair and also has a tendency to provoke scalp sensitisation, irritation or allergy effects.

> **TIP BOX**
>
> Neutralising solutions contain hydrogen peroxide, and so adequate precautions must be taken when using them (see hydrogen peroxide, page 90).

7 Always use separate sponges for the application of permanent waving and neutralising solutions. These sponges should be washed separately and kept in separate containers in between use so that there is no risk of contamination. Use different-coloured sponges for the different processes to avoid confusion.

8 When the processing time is complete, rinse the hair thoroughly to ensure that all traces of the perm solution are removed. A careful rinse lasting no less than three minutes is recommended.

9 After rinsing, it is important to ensure that the hair is reasonably dry before applying the neutralising solution. Each curler must be patted dry with an absorbent towel. Absorbent paper towels and/or cottonwool can be used afterwards to remove as much water as possible. This is to ensure that the neutralising solution is not diluted and thus made less effective by excessive water retained in the hair on the curlers.

10 It is advisable to complete the treatment using the shampoos and conditioners made to complement the brand of permanent waving solution and neutraliser selected. The conditioner, particularly, will act to fortify the stabilisation of the linkages in the hair after the permanent waving treatment is complete.

11 The hairdresser must ask the client if they have had any recent medical illnesses or drug therapies, as these could have a bearing on the successful outcome of the treatment. For example, a person suffering from arthritis may have a high level of uric acid in the hair shaft and this could affect the treatment. Some firms produce a pre-perming lotion for use in these cases. Many drugs, too, will leave deposits in the hair shaft which can affect the treatment, and the hairdresser needs to be aware of these. Every aspect of a client's health is reflected in the hair to a greater or lesser degree. Ideally, perms should not be carried out in the few days before, during and after a woman's menstrual period, as the results of the treatment on the client's hair are less predictable at this time.

Straightening hair

1 The precautions are the same as for permanent waving of hair. However, because the solutions used to straighten hair are stronger, protection of the skin is of prime importance.

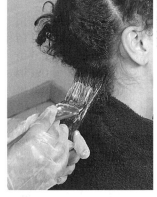

Straightening

2 Because of the stronger solution used, the hair should be combed very gently, and pulling kept to a minimum in order to avoid breakage.

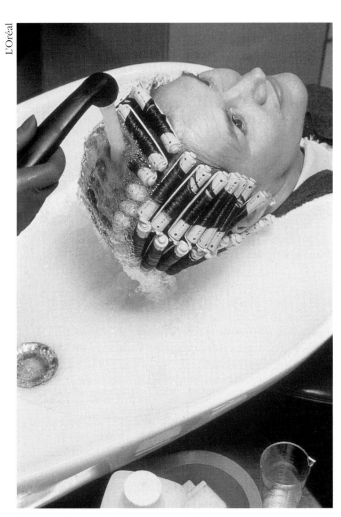

Rinsing the hair prior to neutralisation

• • • • • • CONTRAINDICATIONS • • • • • •

Do not carry out chemical hair treatments of any kind where:

– there is any scalp damage, abrasion, redness or irritation
– the hair is in such poor condition that it will not be able to withstand the use of the relevant chemicals
– Selsun, a proprietary, non-prescription shampoo containing **selenium sulphide**, a substance thought to act as an anti-dandruff agent, or any other shampoo containing this chemical has been used on the hair during the previous 48 hours. This shampoo and other products containing this chemical must also not be used for 48 hours following a chemical hair treatment

– compound henna or other surface-coating metallic dyes are present in the hair. This can include hair-colour restoring products and metallic lacquers – do a strand test first to check.

Hydrogen peroxide

Hydrogen peroxide is used in perming, neutralising, decolouring, colouring, and bleaching processes. It is a highly reactive chemical and care should be taken in its use.

Be aware of the dual terminology applied to hydrogen peroxide concentrations. The original British system refers to peroxide strengths in volumes; the new European system uses percentages. Both are available and a comparison of the two systems is given below.

10 volume is equal in strength to 3%
20 volume is equal in strength to 6%
30 volume is equal in strength to 9%
40 volume is equal in strength to 12%
50 volume is equal in strength to 15%
60 volume is equal in strength to 18%

• • • • • • • • DANGERS • • • • • • • •

Fires; explosion; scalp, skin and eye burns; hair breakage; corrosion of any materials with which it comes into contact, except pottery and glass.

• • • • • • • PRECAUTIONS • • • • • • • •

1 The maximum strength of hydrogen peroxide recommended for use in the salon is 9% (30 volume).
2 If you run out of, for example, 6% hydrogen peroxide, it is not advisable to assume that adding 1 part of 30% hydrogen peroxide to 4 parts of water will give you the required 6%. Likewise, with the old volume measurements, if you run out of 20 volume peroxide, it is not advisable to assume that a 50% dilution of 40 volume peroxide will give you the 20 volume peroxide that you require. In salon conditions, producing peroxide dilutions can be a haphazard and inaccurate process. If it becomes necessary to carry out such a dilution procedure, you must use a piece of equipment known as a hydrometer or peroxometer to obtain the correct strength of peroxide that is required.

3 Hydrogen peroxide is corrosive and will burn skin and clothing if it comes into contact with them. The extent of burning depends on the strength of the peroxide and the length of time of contact. Monitor the condition of the client's skin when using hydrogen peroxide, and flush immediately with large quantities of water if there is any reaction. Be especially careful to keep hydrogen peroxide away from the eyes and ears (see first aid, pages 100 and 106).

TIP BOX

Never mix hydrogen peroxide in metallic bowls or with metallic utensils as contact with metal speeds up the reaction time

4 Hydrogen peroxide is an oxidant. As such, it can spontaneously burst into flames if allowed to dry out on inflammable materials such as paper, wood or hair. Therefore, clean up spilled product and mixtures containing hydrogen peroxide immediately.
5 Hydrogen peroxide must only be used as directed with products which are compatible. If mixed with unsuitable products, it can form dangerous explosive substances.
6 Unused hydrogen peroxide must never be put back into its original container as this can result in decomposition of the rest of the peroxide in the container, altering its strength, and giving off heat and oxygen which could result in an explosion.
7 Never burn hydrogen peroxide – it will explode.

TIP BOX

Do not smoke or have a flame of any kind near hydrogen peroxide or mixtures containing hydrogen peroxide.

8 Store hydrogen peroxide in a cool place out of the sun and away from any heat source. It should be kept in a cupboard which will withstand fire for half an hour or more. In the event of a fire, you must make sure the fire brigade know the quantity, storage conditions and position of these materials.

9 Never store hydrogen peroxide in containers other than those in which it was delivered or dark glass (non-actinic, light-excluding) bottles. It may corrode other containers.

10 The top on the container of hydrogen peroxide must be kept on tightly when not in use. If air is allowed free access to the peroxide, it will cause the peroxide to decompose into water and oxygen, thus weakening the strength of the solution.

Lice (pediculus humanus capitis)

A head louse

S. Lewis

Head lice are small creatures about the size of a pin head, with six short stubby legs at the front of their body that are specially adapted for holding on to the hair shaft. They live on hair near the scalp where they find food and warmth. They are very difficult to see as they hide when the hair is parted, and their colour blends in with that of the scalp. The pearly white, small, oval structures which hairdressers are taught to look for prior to shampooing, commonly called nits and found in clusters attached to the hair shafts, are actually the empty egg shells of newly hatched lice.

Head lice feed on blood, using their specially developed mouth parts to pierce the scalp. As they bite, they inject a local anaesthetic into the scalp so the bite is not felt. They also produce an anticoagulant to stop the blood from clotting, making it easier for them to feed. The bite, anticoagulant and anaesthetic are all causes of allergic and other reactions to the lice.

Each louse takes 14 days to mature and be able to lay eggs. They live for up to 30 days. Once mature, they lay 6–8 eggs per day, gluing them in clusters to the hair shafts. The eggs take 7–10 days to hatch.

Head lice cannot jump or fly and can only live on a human head, not in bedding, clothes, pets or furniture. The only way they can be passed on is by literally walking

A nit

BLM Health

from one head to another. This is why lice are so common in schools, where children often lean their heads together.

• • • • • • • • • DANGERS • • • • • • • • •

An itchy reaction to the bites of the lice, like a mosquito or midge bite; an allergy reaction to the bites with redness, swelling, itching and possible weeping and breakage of the scalp; infestation of other people.

• • • • • • • • PRECAUTIONS • • • • • • • •

The only way head lice can be prevented is by avoiding hair-to-hair contact with an infected person. Insecticides *should not* be used as a preventative treatment.

One of the reasons for combing a client's hair prior to shampooing is to check for head lice. Using a fine-toothed comb, the hair should be parted in various places over the head, paying particular attention to the areas above the ears and towards the nape of the neck, all the time looking for either moving lice or the tell-tale white 'nits' (empty egg cases) sticking to the base of the hair shafts. If lice are found:

1 The client should be quietly and courteously informed by a senior member of staff. They should not be made to feel ashamed – lice have no preference for clean or dirty hair.
2 The client should be told how to treat and eradicate the problem. It may be useful for the salon to have a printed help sheet containing this information which the client can take home (see first aid, page 111).
3 The client must leave the salon to avoid passing on the infestation to others.
4 Every single item with which the client has been in contact must be thoroughly cleansed with a strong disinfectant or antibacterial solution. Small items which can be soaked, e.g. combs, towels, coathanger and gown, must be soaked in a strong disinfectant solution for no less than 20 minutes. Larger items, e.g. chairs, cubicle walls and floors, must be thoroughly washed down with a similar solution.
5 Members of staff who attended to the client must shower, scrub their nails, change their clothes and treat their own hair in a way suitable for killing any infestation. The clothes which were worn while attending to the client must also be disinfected.

Plaiting, weaving, beading and extensions

• • • • • • • • DANGERS • • • • • • • •

Hair breakage, traction baldness, scalp lesions.

Weaving

• • • • • • • PRECAUTIONS • • • • • • • •

1 Avoid pulling the plaiting, weaving, beading or extension stems too tightly during the treatment as this can cause discomfort and headaches. Sometimes a client will experience a small amount of discomfort for a few hours after the treatment until the hair becomes used to the new direction of styling. If this occurs, the client should return to the hairdresser for help.

2 Repeated plaiting, beading, weaving or wearing of extensions, and leaving these styles in for too long (e.g. weeks or months at a time), can cause traction baldness and hair breakage.

3 As the wearing of tight plaiting, beading, weaving and extensions can be damaging to the hair, this needs to be discussed with clients before treatment so that they can be free to make their own decisions regarding these styles. The damage is directly proportional to the length of time the style is worn, the care given to the style, and the weakness of the hair.

Posture

• • • • • • • • DANGERS • • • • • • • •

Poor working posture can lead to problems, aches and pains in the neck and shoulders, lower back and knees. These in turn can sometimes lead to headaches, problems in the hands, and sciatica. Long periods of standing can contribute towards the formation of varicose veins.

• • • • • • • PRECAUTIONS • • • • • • •

The human frame was never designed to work for long periods with the arms held in front of the body, curving the shoulders forward and putting strain on the trapezius muscles across the top of the shoulders; nor with the head inclined forward, throwing the considerable weight of the head on to the muscles of the neck. Ideally, the ears, shoulders, hips and ankles should be held in a straight line at right angles to the floor. Hairdressers will be unable to maintain this ideal posture for much of the time due to the nature of their work, so compensatory actions have to be taken. (See also back care and lifting, page 21.)

1 Try to participate in some form of physical activity in which movement of the upper body is pronounced, e.g. swimming, as a hobby outside of working hours.

> **TIP BOX**
>
> The stomach muscles work in close connection to the lower back muscles. Exercises done to strengthen the stomach muscles will indirectly and gently also strengthen the lower back muscles.

2 During working hours, stretch and rotate the neck, shoulders and arms two or three times a day to maintain flexibility.

3 Use a stool on castors to sit on when working on the client's lower head and neck, especially when cutting.

4 If prone to varicose veins or knee problems, wear support stockings for work.

5 After work, try to rest with the legs above the head for 10–15 minutes to prevent or relieve swelling of the legs and varicose veins.

6 Consider having a regular monthly, or more frequent, massage. This will help to improve the blood circulation, eliminate muscular spasms and keep the joints in a healthy condition.

7 Shoes with arch supports and a small heel will help maintain the correct body posture.

Shampooing

• • • • • • • • DANGERS • • • • • • • • •

Allergies (to the shampoo), scratching the scalp, scalds, tangling and pulling out the hair, falls due to slipping on wet floors, eczema on the hands of the shampooist.

• • • • • • • PRECAUTIONS • • • • • • • •

I Always use good quality shampoos in the salon. Select ones that contain few allergy-provoking agents (e.g. perfumes). If the client experiences any burning or stinging sensation, the shampoo should be rinsed away immediately and not

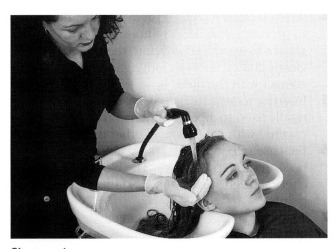

Shampooing

used again. This should be noted on the client's record card.

2 The shampooist's nails should be kept short – certainly no longer than the length of the end of the fingers.

3 The shampooist should not wear any rings as these may catch and scratch the client's scalp (a smooth wedding ring is acceptable).

TIP BOX

Examine the hair for lice, check the scalp for abrasions or rashes, and comb out any knots before shampooing.

4 The wetting and rinsing waters should always be tested by the shampooist before allowing them to come into contact with the client's head. Even then, the client must be asked if the temperature is agreeable, as different people have different thresholds of sensation.

5 The shampoo should always be dispensed on to the shampooist's hands before placing it on the client's head. Cold shampoo tipped directly on to a warm head can give quite an unpleasant shock, especially to elderly clients of nervous disposition.

6 Use an efficient shampooing technique, which does not pull and tangle the hair whether it is long or short, at all times.

7 The shampooing area should be designed so that splashing and spillage of water are eliminated as far as possible. A cloth or mop should also be kept readily at hand to deal with any spillage before it can cause an accident.

8 To help keep the possibility of falls to a minimum, it is advisable to provide a non-slip floor covering in the 'wet' areas of the salon.

9 The shampooist should take care to dry their hands thoroughly after every treatment as perpetually damp hands contribute to skin eczema. Long-lasting barrier products are available to protect the skin of the hands through many shampoos, and these should be made available and worn as a preventative measure. A shampooist with a tendency to eczema should wear well-fitting protective gloves while shampooing.

•••••CONTRAINDICATIONS•••••••

- a broken or infected scalp
- redness and soreness of the scalp
- pest infestations, e.g. lice (see page 91)

Care must also be taken around any recent cuts or abrasions.

Steamers

••••••••DANGERS•••••••••

Scalds, electric shock.

A steamer

•••••••PRECAUTIONS••••••••

1 Ensure that the stand is firm and that the equipment is not in a position where either the client or a member of the staff can knock it over. (See also electrical equipment, page 26.)
2 Ensure that the hood is evenly placed over the head so that the steam is evenly distributed.
3 Stay within sight of the client during the steaming process. It is important that clients can contact you quickly if they are in any difficulty, and that you can watch to see that they are all right.
4 Ensure that the water level in the equipment is maintained at recommended levels. If the level falls too much, it may 'over-boil' during the treatment, resulting in boiling water spitting out on to the client.

Wig (postiche) cleaning and making – human hair

•••••••••DANGERS•••••••••

Fainting, unconsciousness, possible death, potential fire hazard.

••••••••PRECAUTIONS•••••••

As detergents and water would cause the deterioration of both the human hair and the base into which this is woven, a dry-cleaning agent, trichloroethylene (previously known as carbon tetrachloride), is often used to clean human hair wigs. Sometimes other less dangerous solvents are used, but they are still flammable and toxic, so the same precautions apply.

This section does not apply to the more modern synthetic wigs now manufactured, as these have their own, less dangerous, cleaning methods.

1 Trichloroethylene and other cleaning solvents are highly inflammable and should not be used near a naked flame or while smoking.
2 Trichloroethylene and other cleaning solvents are extremely toxic. If used in an enclosed, unventilated space, the fumes are capable of causing death. Therefore, these solvent chemicals must be used very sparingly and in a large, mechanically ventilated room. The wigs must be left to 'air' in a mechanically ventilated room or outside for some hours after cleaning.
3 In between use, the solvent chemicals must be kept in a strong lock-up cupboard so that they cannot be used for anything other than dry-cleaning purposes.
4 When using the solvents, a mask must be worn to prevent inhalation of fumes, protective glasses to avoid splashes into the eyes, and gloves and protective clothing to prevent bodily contact with the fluid.
5 In order to avoid accidents, hackles should be rigidly fixed to a bench when in use and covered with a guard at all other times.
6 For ease of handling, hackles and blocks should be stored on low shelves. The blocks should be checked regularly to remove unnecessary block points.
7 To avoid damage to both handler and tools, care must be taken when handling or storing knotting hooks.

PART THREE

First aid in the salon

First aid in the salon

Falls, fits, burns, insect bites and asthma attacks, to name but a few problems, can happen to anyone, anywhere. Because of this, it is in everyone's interest to have a basic knowledge of first aid so that assistance can be given in a time of need.

Beauty therapists and hairdressers must be able to deal promptly with any eventuality arising at their place of work, be it a fainting spell or a heart attack. In many cases, the therapist or hairdresser will be in the unfortunate position of having inflicted the injury on the client in the first place. An over-generous application of eyelash tint, or a moment's lack of concentration while using hot curling tongs or a hand dryer, are simple examples of potential hazards.

Therapists and hairdressers also need to be aware of measures they can take to protect themselves from any harm which could result from a casualty or accident, e.g. blood-borne infections or electric shock.

However, it is not the therapist's or hairdresser's place to *treat* an injury or condition, but only to apply *first aid* and make sure that the affected person receives treatment from others properly qualified to give it, e.g. a doctor or nurse. In offering unqualified, though well meant, treatment, you might put the casualty's life at risk. For example, an aspirin given to someone complaining of a headache could provoke a strong allergic reaction; and burn cream or lavender oil applied to a burn could hinder medical treatment of the condition. With the exceptions of applying calamine lotion to mild sunburn, giving sugar to a diabetic and supplying a single aspirin to chew in the event of a heart attack, anyone providing first aid *must never* take responsibility for administering any drug, cream, oil, or substance other than plain water to the casualty. Even a drink is forbidden if it is thought that the casualty might need an operation, as this would delay the use of a general anaesthetic for vital hours!

This may seem harsh to therapists who are used to using alternative remedies to treat themselves at home, but the first-aider must realise that if anything goes wrong because of their incorrect treatment of the casualty, they are then vulnerable to a claim by the injured party. Insurance cover for anyone administering first aid is only valid if the correct emergency procedure as set down in the authorised first-aid manuals has been followed. Even on the street, the 'Good Samaritan' principle will support people acting in an emergency only if they do not stray beyond the accepted first-aid boundaries. In other words, apply first aid because you may be able to save a person's life, but leave second aid and treatment to properly qualified medical people.

Knowledge of correct first-aid procedures is clearly vital, both for the sake of the casualty and for the protection of the hairdresser or therapist.

This part of the book lists, in alphabetical order, each injury or health problem which could conceivably arise in a hairdressing or therapy workplace. A description of its symptoms is followed by the correct first-aid procedure that should be administered until qualified medical help can be obtained.

Although it is not legally necessary for a hairdresser or beauty therapist to possess any first-aid qualification, emergency first-aid training should be considered by all. Various voluntary organisations run courses in first aid, in night-school or daytime format, which are open to anyone who is interested. The three main organisations which run training courses are, The St John Ambulance, The St Andrew's Ambulance Association, and The British Red Cross Society. Each of these organisations is listed in the telephone directory and will supply details of their courses on request.

Allergy reactions and rashes

If an allergy reaction occurs during a treatment, it can be immediately identified by the appearance of excessive redness and possibly swelling, vesicle formation, itching, or a severe burning sensation in the area of the application of a product.

• • • • • • • • • **FIRST AID** • • • • • • • • •

Remove the product immediately with quantities of plain tap water. If necessary, apply cold compresses or a cold pack (see page 101) to the affected area. If the reaction does not subside completely, refer the casualty to a doctor immediately. Tell the doctor which product caused the reaction.

The product and details of the reaction it caused must be entered on the client's record card and never used on that client again.

If the client returns to the salon with a suspected allergy rash some time after the treatment has been given, they should be referred to a doctor immediately as this may be a sign of unexpected complications, e.g. infection of the rash. Doctors are also equipped to identify the source of the allergy. It may not be due to a product you have used in the salon.

Artificial ventilation

If the casualty has stopped breathing, the first-aider must breathe for them using artificial ventilation.

There are several methods of artificial ventilation, the most effective being mouth-to-mouth. This is a technique which needs to be demonstrated and practised on special models rather than learned from a book. The St John Ambulance Centres, St Andrew's Ambulance Association and British Red Cross Society run regular short courses on first aid and it is advisable to attend one of these to learn how to perform mouth-to-mouth ventilation correctly. However, the following information is provided as a reminder of how this technique should be performed in an emergency.

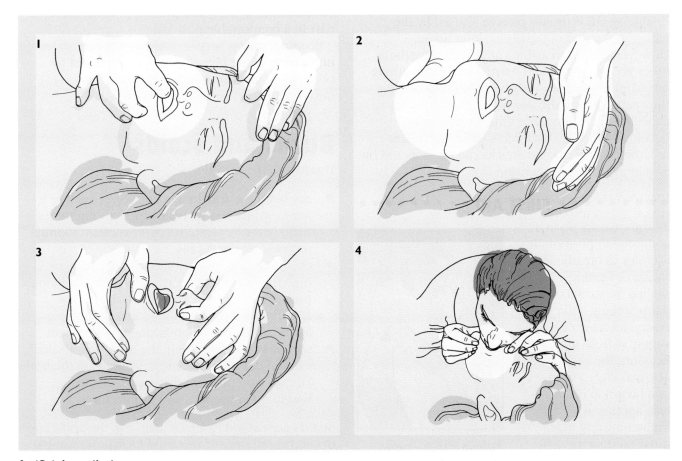

Artificial ventilation

1 Make sure that nothing is blocking or constricting the airway.

2 Tilt the head well back to open the air passages.

3 Pinch the casualty's nose closed.

4 Take a deep breath, seal your lips around the casualty's mouth, and blow until you see their chest rise.

5 Take your mouth away and allow their chest to fall.

6 Continue at a rate of 10 breaths per minute. Check the pulse every 10 breaths.

If the heart has stopped, i.e. there is no pulse, artificial ventilation needs to be combined with chest compressions (see page 101). Together they are known as cardio-pulmonary resuscitation or CPR. To administer CPR, the ratio is:

- with one first-aider, 2 breaths every 15 compressions
- with two first-aiders, 1 breath every 5 compressions

Asthma

Breathing out is usually passive, caused by the natural retraction of the elastic lung tissue. However, during an asthma attack, the breathing tubes go into spasm and narrow so that breathing out naturally and passively becomes impossible, thus necessitating the use of the chest muscles to expel the air. At the same time, breathing in becomes difficult. This forced, difficult, wheezy breathing is asthma and attacks can be triggered by an allergy or nervous tension.

● ● ● ● ● ● ● ● ● **FIRST AID** ● ● ● ● ● ● ● ● ●

Sit the casualty up in a comfortable position. It is easier to breathe if sitting or leaning slightly forward. Loosen tight clothing and ensure an adequate supply of fresh air. Reassure the casualty. The inability to release one breath in order to take another is frightening and may cause panic, especially if it is a first attack. If

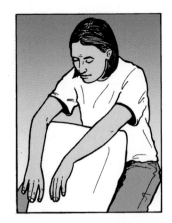

Asthma attack – make the casualty comfortable

they have their personal medication with them, let them use it. If the attack persists, is severe, or is a first attack, call for an ambulance.

Bruises

A bruise is the result of bleeding into tissues beneath the skin after a fall or knock. A bruise will swell more if it is over a bony area, e.g. the shin, but this does not mean that it is a more severe bruise, it just looks worse. A normal bruise is blue/black and looks swollen at first. It fades over a matter of days becoming yellowish and then disappearing altogether.

Bruising can develop very slowly, appearing hours or days after injury. However, rapidly developing bruising which appears to be the main problem will benefit from first aid.

● ● ● ● ● ● ● ● ● **FIRST AID** ● ● ● ● ● ● ● ● ●

If the area is very painful and swollen, both the pain and swelling can be reduced by the application of a cold compress for at least 20 minutes. This can be done in four ways (see cold compresses, page 101). For all of them, first raise and support the affected part in a comfortable position.

Bruising, unless very severe and with extensive underlying tissue bleeding, or accompanied by other worrying symptoms, e.g. shock (page 115), needs no further medical attention.

Burns and scalds

Burns can be caused by:

- dry heat, e.g. touching a hot object such as a flame, sauna heater, heat lamp, curling tongs, hand dryer or cigarette; overexposure to infra-red or ultra-violet rays
- electricity, e.g. contact with the tweezers used in high-frequency epilation; excess current being passed through the short-wave diathermy needle; contact with faulty salon equipment, lights or plugs; or high-frequency treatment
- corrosive chemicals, e.g. the acids and alkalis formed during a galvanic treatment on the body, face, or for epilation; dyes and bleaches; undiluted antiseptics and disinfectants.

Scalds are caused by moist heat, e.g. the application of overheated organic wax used for hair removal; the application of overheated paraffin wax also used for hair removal or for therapeutic reasons; steam baths; sauna (placing the water on the hot coals); the spillage of hot drinks; showers; boiling water; facial steamers; poultices applied when they are too hot; manicure and pedicure bowls containing oil or water which is too hot; and hair rinsing water which is too hot.

All burns and scalds are accompanied by redness and swelling. More severe injuries lead to swelling, blistering and, in severe cases, charring. There is also a danger of shock, especially in burns which have broken the skin or cover large areas.

All burns and scalds cause intense pain. A shallow injury will be more painful than a deep one. With a shallow burn or scald, the nerve endings are stimulated into action, whereas with a deep burn, the nerve endings are destroyed.

However, it is not the depth of a burn which is most important, but the area which it covers. The dangers of shock are directly related to the extent of the injury and any casualty severely burned or scalded must be taken to hospital as soon as the appropriate first aid has been administered.

An example of a severe injury would be a wax-inflicted scald with an area in excess of 5 cm by 3.5 cm, or one which begins to blister. Use your judgement *very carefully* in these matters. Remember, it is not the therapist's place to treat an injury, only to apply first aid and then refer the injured party for treatment by a qualified person. However, minor burns or scalds can usually be alleviated by the immediate administration of the correct first-aid procedures.

• • • • • • • • • FIRST AID • • • • • • • • • •

Emergency procedure in the event of a fire

1 Send for the fire brigade.
2 Remove casualties from danger if it is safe to do so.
3 Do not enter a burning building or a smoke or fume-filled room.

If someone is on fire

1 Do not let them run outdoors.
2 Lay them down, burning side uppermost, and throw water on them *or* wrap them tightly in a coat or rug to smother the flames.

Checklist for all burns

1 If severe, send for medical help *first,*
2 Flush with cold water for 10 minutes. Remove tight items.

3 Do not remove anything stuck to the burn or pierce blisters.
4 Cover with clean, light, dry, non-fluffy material and seek medical help if necessary and you have not already done so.
5 If severe, lay the casualty down, raise their legs, and check their breathing and pulse every 10 minutes until medical help arrives.

TIP BOX

Bacteria can go through wet material but not dry. If dry, non-fluffy material is not available, use a clean plastic bag or a clean piece of clingfilm to cover the burn. *Never* put the dressing on tightly – allow for swelling. *Never* use a plaster as this might remove skin when taken off.

Scalds and dry-heat burns

The first priority is to cool down the injured area by flushing with cold water for at least 10 minutes, or until the pain subsides. Do this in the most efficient way possible. For a hand or arm injury, place the area under a *slow* running cold-water tap. For a leg injury, use a bath if you have one, filled with cold water. For a body injury, again a bath or a cold shower (running slowly) would be ideal. Failing these, use a basin of cold water and constantly splash or immerse the area. This serves to stop the spread of heat in the tissues, thus minimising the damage and also relieving the pain.

If a scald has been caused by a spilled hot drink, hold the hot saturated clothing away from the body *immediately*, removing it if possible, while someone goes for cold water or while taking the client to a source of cold water.

If the casualty is wearing anything tight in the area of the burn, e.g. a watch, ring or bangle, remove this immediately before swelling starts.

If blisters occur, they must not be broken or cut away, as they serve to prevent the entry of infection into the wound.

If anything is stuck to the burn, e.g. wax, burned clothing, melted plastic or singed hair, it must not be removed.

Dress the injury with a dry, lightweight, clean, non-fluffy material, e.g. a burns sheet, clean non-fluffy fabric or kitchen film. A lint dressing would leave bits of lint sticking to the injury when removed. (If lint is all that is available, use the reverse side which is not fluffy.) The main aim is to protect the wound against infection. Any adhesion between the dressing and the skin is undesirable. Do not apply any oils, creams, fats or ointments as these only create difficulty when they have to be removed by the medical person who will give the follow-up treatment.

If necessary, arrange for the casualty to go to a hospital for correct medical treatment. If the burn is severe, get medical help *swiftly*.

Scalp burns from a hair dryer

It is not very practical to saturate the client's hair and head with cold water, but this must be done if the need arises, e.g. for a large burn. If the burn is small, the area must still be cooled as quickly and as efficiently as possible. To do this, it is best to apply a cold compress to the area (see page 101) for approximately 10 minutes before continuing to treat as normal for a dry-heat burn (see checklist, page 99).

Corrosive chemical burns

When the burns are due to chemical hair treatments such as **perming and bleaching**, the area must be flushed with plenty of plain, cold water, but care must be taken to protect yourself from the corrosive chemicals and any toxic fumes which may be present, and to ensure that the contaminated water can drain away safely. Treat as a burn (see checklist, page 99).

During **galvanic electrolysis**, burns can be caused by sodium hydroxide which is produced under the skin by this method. This must be neutralised by the application of roller cataphoresis, (the roller connected to the positive pole) for 2–3 minutes. Further action depends on the severity of the injury. Apply first aid as for a burn (see checklist, page 99).

Surface burns from **galvanic treatment** are caused by the concentrations of acid and alkali produced during the treatment. They appear as a string of grey dots or a large grey area. They are deep and cause the tissue to break away. They heal very slowly. As for any burn, flush with lots of cold water for at least 10 minutes. Apply a clean, light, non-fluffy, dry dressing and seek immediate medical attention. Sometimes there is no apparent damage after the treatment, but blisters arise later. The client must be told not to break the blisters, but to apply a clean, dry dressing and seek immediate medical aid.

If **eyelash tint** enters the eye, treat as for any chemical burn (see above). Flush the eye with cool running water from the tap or a glass or rinsing bottle for at least 10 minutes before covering with a pad of clean, non-fluffy material and seeking medical attention. (See also eye injuries, page 106.)

Undiluted antiseptics and disinfectants can produce severe skin burns, and can be seen when a person has incorrectly bathed recently pierced ears with an undiluted antiseptic or disinfectant solution. In such cases, refer the client to the doctor with a note straight away. (See also ear piercing, page 105.) In cases of accidental contact with undiluted antiseptics or disinfectants in the salon, flush the area with large quantities of cold water immediately to dilute the solution and apply first aid as for a burn (see checklist, page 99).

Electrical burns

These can range from tiny high-frequency sparking burns to deeper high-frequency tweezer burns, and even to the far more severe burns from mains current electrocution caused by contact with faulty electrical equipment (see electric shock, page 105).

For very minor electrical burns such as might be caused by tweezer epilation equipment, do nothing except inform your client of the damage and advise them to seek medical advice if it becomes necessary.

However, if you are in any doubt, the injury should be treated as if it were serious. The area should be cooled with water for at least 10 minutes, a dry dressing applied, and the client sent for medical attention. Although it is usually the area of a burn, not the depth, which is most critical, electrical burns are always very much deeper than their size indicates.

TIP BOX

Burn ointments, gels, oils and creams should never be used during first-aid procedures.

Overexposure to infra-red heat

This should be treated as a normal dry-heat burn – flush with lots of cold water for at least 10 minutes, apply a clean, dry dressing, and arrange for the casualty to go to hospital for correct medical treatment. Burns from infra-red lamps can cover large areas, so great care must be taken to see that the casualty does not go into shock (see page 115).

Overexposure to ultra-violet rays

There is little that can be done to counteract overexposure to ultra-violet rays from a solarium. In mild cases, the immediate application of infra-red to erythema level serves to counteract some of the damage. However, the extent of the damage cannot be seen for some 6–8 hours. It is vital that the casualty sees a doctor straight away for correct medical care.

Conjunctivitis can arise from failing to wear eye protection while undergoing sunbed treatment. Advise the casualty to bathe the eyes with cool, pure water frequently. If the condition does not clear up within 24 hours, medical advice must be sought.

Overexposure to UVA rays (sunbeds) can result in severe irritation and itching. Further sunbed treatment or sunbathing must be avoided until all sensitivity has disappeared. The client must then be carefully monitored through subsequent treatments.

Chest compressions

If there is no pulse, the heart has stopped. However, blood can be made to circulate by performing chest compressions.

As with artificial ventilation, this is a technique which needs to be demonstrated and practised on special models rather than learned from a book. The St John Ambulance Centres, St Andrew's Ambulance Association and British Red Cross Society run regular short courses on first aid and it is advisable to attend one of these to learn how to perform chest compressions correctly. However, the following information is provided as a reminder of how this technique should be performed in an emergency.

1. Lay the casualty flat on their back on a firm surface.
2. Place the heel of one hand two finger widths above the point where the casualty's bottom ribs meet the breastbone. Place the heel of the other hand over it and interlock your fingers.
3. Press vertically down on the breastbone with straight arms to depress their chest by 4–5 cm.
4. Release the pressure and repeat at a rate of approximately 80 per minute (count one and two and three, etc.).

Chest compressions need to be combined with artificial ventilation (see page 97) in order to

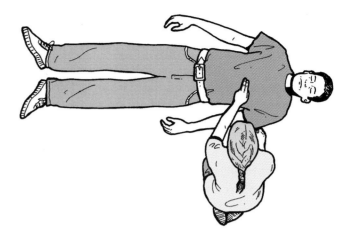

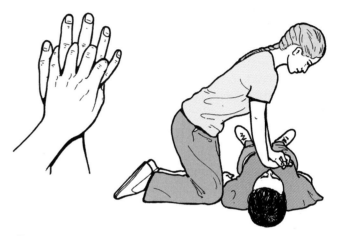

Chest compressions

oxygenate the blood. The two techniques used together are known as cardio-pulmonary resuscitation or CPR. To administer CPR, the ratio is:

- with one first-aider, 2 breaths every 15 compressions
- with two first-aiders, 1 breath every 5 compressions.

Cold compresses

Cooling injuries such as bruises, sprains and strains will help minimise swelling and pain. Cooling is also beneficial for headaches, insect stings and any swellings or inflammation.

Cold compresses can take different forms depending on what is available and where the injury is on the body. They can be applied in four ways:

1. Place the injured part directly under cold running water or in a bowl of cold water.

2 Use cold tap water to soak an absorbent towel or similar. Wring out the towel just enough so that it is not dripping, then place it on the injury. Resoak the towel every five minutes to keep it cool. If necessary, hold it in place with an open-weave bandage which will allow the water to evaporate and cool the area. Cool the injured part for at least 20 minutes.

3 If a freezer and ice is available, an ice pack can be made by filling a plastic bag half to two-thirds full of crushed ice. Squeeze the air out of the bag, tie and wrap in a thin towel. Apply to the injury.

4 A useful addition to any salon is a coolpack, to be kept in a freezer. These are flexible sealed bags containing a fluid with an extremely low freezing point. As well as being useful during treatments such as underarm waxing, they make ideal cold compresses in case of accidents. They should be wrapped in a thin towel before use.

Cramp

Cramp is a sudden, involuntary, painful muscle contraction. It can be caused by poor circulation, e.g. insufficient warming up before an exercise class, or by loss of salt and body fluids through excessive perspiration.

• • • • • • • • **FIRST AID** • • • • • • • •

1 Wherever the cramp occurs, stretch the muscle as much as you can and massage it.

2 If the cramp is in the calf muscles, get the casualty to stand on the affected leg, straighten the knee and press the heel down into the floor as hard as possible. Massage the muscles.

3 If the cramp is in the toes, get the casualty to stand on the ball of the foot and press the foot forwards. When the first spasm has passed, massage the foot.

4 If the cramp is in the fingers, straighten the fingers and massage them well.

5 For cramp in the back of the thigh, straighten the knee and massage the muscles firmly. For cramp in the front of the thigh, bend the knee and massage the muscles firmly.

6 If stretching and massaging the muscle has no beneficial effect on the cramp and the casualty has been perspiring profusely prior to the attack (e.g. as a result of jogging or exertion at an exercise class), the cramp could be due to loss of body salt content. In such instances the casualty should drink half a teaspoonful of salt dissolved in a litre of water. This will replace the fluids and salt lost and relieve the cramp attack. (See also heat exhaustion, page 109.)

Cuts

In a hairdressing and beauty salon, the most common causes of minor cuts are from cuticle clipping, eyebrow tweezing and scissors. Often hairdressers and therapists inflict these accidentally on themselves. (Scissors tucked into a pocket can be particularly dangerous.)

Whatever the nature of the cut, first-aiders must protect themselves from contracting any blood-borne infections. This can be done by wearing protection, e.g. rubber gloves, or avoiding direct contact with blood. Always keep any of your own cuts or sores covered with waterproof plasters and wash your hands thoroughly with soap and water before and after treating the casualty.

The cut itself must be kept clean to prevent the entry of infection, and any blood loss should be controlled or stopped by applying pressure over the wound and raising the injured part. If there is a foreign body in the wound or the wound is particularly at risk of infection, e.g. a puncture by a dirty object or a bite, seek medical advice.

• • • • • • • • **FIRST AID** • • • • • • • •

Minor cuts

1 Cleanse the area if necessary by rinsing lightly under running water. Soap and water can be used to clean the surrounding area.

2 If bleeding occurs (in the case of a cuticle injury this is usual), apply a small

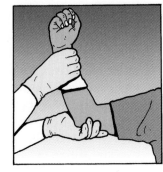

Bleeding – apply pressure to the wound

TIP BOX

All the above movements can also be carried out with the casualty in the lying down position.

pad of clean cottonwool or sterile gauze to the area. Hold it in place and apply pressure for 2–4 minutes while at the same time keeping the injured area elevated. The bleeding should stop after this time. If it does not, the cut is more severe and may need medical attention.

3 Cover the cut with a dry adhesive dressing (plaster) to keep it clean and prevent the entry of infection.

Deep cuts

Any cut which penetrates the entire thickness of the skin and leaves the edges of the skin gaping slightly must be covered with a sterile dressing and seen by a doctor immediately. Any cut on the face must be attended to by a doctor because of the risk of scarring in this area.

If the bleeding is heavy, stop it with direct pressure on top of or above the wound, using your hand or fingers and a pad made from a sterile dressing or clean fabric. At the same time, elevate the wound. Bleeding should stop within 10 minutes. When it does, apply a clean dressing and bandage firmly. If there is anything in the wound, e.g. glass or wood, do not put the dressing immediately over the top of this, but make a ring out of another bandage and place this over the area before bandaging in order to keep the pressure off the foreign body. Do not attempt to remove a foreign body from a wound. If blood oozes through the dressing, do not remove it but apply another one on top. Keep the injured limb raised to stem the blood flow until medical assistance arrives.

If simple direct pressure fails to stop the bleeding and the wound is to an arm or a leg, you may be able to stop it by pressing the main artery of the affected limb against a bone. This is always necessary if the damage is to the actual artery and the blood is coming out in spurts. If the injury is to the arm, then pressure must be applied to the brachial artery. This can be found along the inner side of the muscles of

Brachial pressure point. To apply pressure, pass your fingers under the injured party's upper arm and compress the artery against the bone

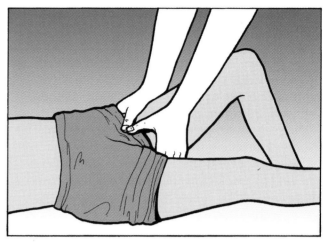

Femoral pressure point. To apply pressure, bend the casualty's knee, firmly hold their thigh with both hands, and press directly and firmly downwards in the centre of the groin with both thumbs, one on top of the other against the rim of the pelvis

the upper arm, its course being roughly indicated by the inner seam of a coat sleeve. If the injury is to the leg, then pressure must be applied to the femoral artery at the centre front (trouser crease) of the fold of the groin. Pressure applied to any of these pressure points must not be maintained for longer than 10 minutes or damage to the limb will result from the lack of blood circulation. For this reason, immediate medical attention should be sought.

Cuts to varicose veins

Bleeding from a varicose vein can be sudden and severe, developing rapidly into shock if not controlled quickly.

Lay the casualty down on their back and raise the injured leg as high as possible. Immediately apply direct pressure over a sterile dressing or clean pad or just with the fingers. Any constrictions impeding blood flow back to the heart, e.g. elastic-topped stockings, should be removed. A pad should be bandaged firmly into position and an ambulance called without delay.

Diabetes

Diabetes mellitus is a complaint caused by the malfunctioning of the mechanisms in the body which regulate the blood sugar level. A severely lowered blood sugar level results in a diabetic coma. To avoid this, diabetics inject themselves with insulin and adhere to a rigid diet to regulate the blood sugar level and keep it within acceptable limits. However, sometimes abnormalities occur. Diabetics may mistakenly inject themselves with too much insulin. They may delay or miss a meal, or use up blood sugar supplies unexpectedly through unusual exercise or a stressful situation. All these will induce a coma.

There are two types of coma, one due to an excess of insulin in the bloodstream causing a low blood sugar level (this is the most common) and one due to a lack of insulin, causing a high blood sugar level.

- **Insulin coma due to too much insulin**. The casualty is pale, sweating, breathing shallowly and has a rapid pulse. They will be confused and often aggressive. These symptoms rapidly develop into a faint or coma.
- **Diabetic coma due to not enough insulin**. The casualty is flushed and breathing deeply. Their breath will smell strongly of nail varnish remover (acetone) and they will pass gradually into a coma.

TIP BOX

Do not worry whether the casualty is suffering from excess or lack of insulin. Treat them in the same way regardless.

• • • • • • • • FIRST AID • • • • • • • •

1 If the casualty is conscious, confirm that they are diabetic.
2 Give the casualty a drink sweetened with two full tablespoons of sugar. Alternatively, give them lumps of sugar, chocolate or sweets to suck, or some sweet food to eat. If they improve dramatically, the problem was excess insulin. Give more sugar to prevent a relapse into a coma, then see how they recover and summon medical aid if necessary. If there is no improvement, the problem is lack of insulin. No harm will have been done by giving them sugar, but they need medical treatment – call for an ambulance straight away.
3 If the casualty is unconscious or is relapsing into unconsciousness, loosen any tight clothing, place in the recovery position (see page 114) and send for an ambulance.

4 Search the casualty for a diabetic identification card, lumps of sugar (which diabetics often carry) or insulin injection marks on the arm, thigh or abdomen. Point these out, along with any other information you may have (e.g. the casualty's name and address, doctor and next of kin, times and symptoms), to the medical help when it arrives.

Dislocations and fractures

Both these injuries have similar symptoms and are treated in the same way until medical help (an ambulance) arrives, so it is easier to discuss them together.

A dislocation occurs when one or more bones at a joint are wrenched out of place. The shoulder joint is the easiest joint to displace, but lower jaw, elbows, thumb and fingers are also easily dislocated.

A fracture can be open, i.e. the skin is broken and the bone exposed to the air, or closed, i.e. although broken, the bone does not break the skin.

The symptoms of fractures and dislocations are:

- sickening or severe pain
- misshapen appearance
- inability to move the injured part without great pain (in cases of dislocation, the joint becomes fixed)
- swelling and bruising.

• • • • • • • • FIRST AID • • • • • • • •

Shock often follows a severe fracture or dislocation, so this must be watched for (see page 115).

Do not move the casualty unnecessarily. Medical attention is needed – you may inflict more damage by interfering. This is especially the case in instances of back or neck pain, or loss of feeling in the hands or feet. Here the casualty may have fractured the spine and if the back or neck is moved it may cause permanent paralysis.

Make the casualty as comfortable as possible with the injury immobilised until medical help arrives. To immobilise a broken arm, place it in a sling and tie a bandage around the arm and body avoiding the injury. To immobilise a broken leg, bandage both legs together at the ankles and knees, then above and below the site of the break. In less severe injuries, cushions or bandages can be used to immobilise the limb. Do not attempt to reset any dislocated joints.

Ear-piercing infections and complaints

Some clients may choose to disregard both the verbal and written aftercare instructions after they have had their ears pierced. Consequently, they can return with a variety of complaints such as:

- skin burns resulting from using undiluted antiseptic as an aftercare solution instead of the recommended aftercare solution
- infections, minor or severe, resulting from not following the aftercare instructions, or inserting cheap earrings too soon after piercing
- closed holes due to removing the earrings when instructed not to do so – this often happens when the client has to go into hospital unexpectedly
- formation of keloids.

• • • • • • • • • **FIRST AID** • • • • • • • • •

Skin burns

Skin burns are often quite severe and can be recognised by darkened and hardened skin in the affected area. The casualty must be told not to pick the scabs. As swelling is usually present, the stud must be removed and the area cleansed with a sterile surgical wipe. Arrangements should be made for the casualty to receive medical treatment immediately. Unpleasant as the burn looks, correct medical treatment will soon stimulate healing and the casualty can have the ears repierced once this is complete in approximately 2–4 weeks.

Infections

Infections can be minor or severe. A minor infection would appear as redness and soreness of the ear with no accompanying swelling. Remove the stud, scrub it in warm soapy water (a new toothbrush or a jewellery cleaning brush is a good tool for this procedure) and then sterilise it using whatever method of sterilisation is adopted by the salon. Thoroughly cleanse the wound with a sterile surgical wipe, removing any pus present. Replace the stud and instruct the client firstly to watch for any swelling, and secondly to return to you daily for a repeat of the same procedure until all soreness has gone. If sudden swelling occurs, advise the client to see a doctor *straight away.*

A severe infection would be one with redness, soreness and swelling. If neglected, the swelling can be extreme, i.e.to the extent that the stud becomes embedded in the inside of the lobe. Clean the area using a sterile surgical wipe. Remove the stud if at all possible and arrange for the casualty to receive medical treatment immediately. Antibiotics will be needed. It is always best to telephone and write a covering letter to the doctor or nurse yourself, to explain the situation and make an immediate appointment. The ear can be repierced when complete healing has taken place.

Closed hole

The closing of the pierced area is definitely not an emergency situation, but one which happens frequently. Complete healing of the hole takes 2–3 weeks and so the area must be treated as an open wound and bathed frequently until fully healed. Repiercing can then be carried out as normal.

Keloids

Keloids usually occur as lumps of tissue at the back of the ear. They are caused by over-regeneration of skin tissue during the healing process. Nothing can be done to prevent them in a susceptible person. If it is known that the client is prone to keloid formation, ear piercing should be avoided. If they do occur and are upsetting the client, advise the client to consult their doctor to see if they can be removed. Usually, though, removal would only result in the formation of more keloids, so a doctor is reluctant to recommend this.

Electric shock

In a salon, electric shock would come from the 240-voltage domestic supply and would probably be due to faulty equipment or wiring. Sometimes the person involved cannot release contact with the current due to muscle spasm or injury.

• • • • • • • • FIRST AID • • • • • • • •

1 Break the electrical contact, i.e. switch off or unplug the appliance or ideally switch off at the mains. If for some reason you cannot do this, then stand on some dry insulating material, e.g. a rubber mat or telephone directory, and attempt to push the casualty away from the contact using something dry and wooden or plastic, e.g. a broom handle. *Do not* touch the casualty with your hands or something wet or the electricity will be passed on, and you will receive a shock too.

2 The shock may stop the casualty's heart or breathing. Be prepared to administer artificial ventilation (see page 97) or CPR.

3 Send for immediate medical aid. Call for an ambulance.

4 Treat the burns if necessary (see page 100). Note: electrical burns are always much deeper than their size indicates.

Epilepsy

Epilepsy is the name given to convulsions or loss of consciousness due to abnormal electrical activity in the brain.

During a minor attack the subject goes pale and their eyes become fixed and staring for a few minutes, completely oblivious to the surroundings. Usually the subject 'comes to' immediately and carries on conversation, unaware that anything has happened. Sometimes a minor attack can take the form of a faint. In both these cases, the casualty may be a little confused after the attack and not totally aware of what they are doing.

A major attack can appear quite frightening, but there is no cause for alarm. Symptoms can be as follows:

- The casualty will suddenly lose consciousness and collapse to the floor.
- For a few seconds, the casualty will remain rigid, perhaps not even breathing and possibly going 'blue in the face' through lack of oxygen.
- Muscle groups will then start to contract and relax alternately (convulsions). The jaw will be clenched, leading to forced, noisy breathing.
- Saliva can appear at the mouth, bloodstained if the tongue has been bitten. Because control of the muscles has been lost, the casualty may be incontinent, i.e. pass urine or faeces involuntarily.
- Suddenly the casualty will relax completely and begin to regain consciousness. They will

remember nothing of the attack and may be confused, embarrassed, and need a while to pull themselves together.

• • • • • • • • • FIRST AID • • • • • • • • •

The aim of any first-aid treatment is to prevent self-injury as a result of lack of control over the body.

1 If you see the casualty falling, try to support them or ease their fall. Remove anything from the vicinity that might injure them, e.g. chairs, glasses, fires, etc. Do not restrain them, just guide their movements so that they are safe. Ask any onlookers to move away.

2 Loosen any clothing around the neck and try to protect their head.

3 Do not place anything into their mouth during the fit. Just keep checking to ensure that the airway is clear and that they can breathe. Wipe away any froth from the mouth.

4 Do not try to restrain the casualty, or lift or move them unless they are in danger, e.g. from a fire.

5 As they relax, place them in the recovery position (see page 114) so that they can breathe properly. Cover them with a blanket for warmth if necessary. Stay with them until they recover fully and are completely aware of what they are doing. Find some clean, dry clothes if they have soiled themselves; try to relieve their embarrassment and calm them down.

6 Advise them to see a doctor or, if it is a first attack or if the casualty is not recovering properly, send for an ambulance.

Eye injuries

There are two major causes of eye injuries in hairdressing and beauty salons: chemicals and foreign bodies. Potentially hazardous chemicals include eyelash dye, perm solution, tinting solution, aromatherapy oils and nail varnish remover. Common foreign bodies in the eye are eyelashes, hair and pieces of grit. Less common but potentially more dangerous are pieces of artificial nail or nail clippings.

• • • • • • • • • FIRST AID • • • • • • • • •

Chemicals in the eye

The aim of first-aid treatment is to dilute the chemical in the eye. This can be done by using large quantities of water.

1 Quickly place the head on its side with the affected eye nearest to the floor. Using the squeezy bottle with a long, flexible tube filled with sterile distilled water which is kept in the first-aid kit, squirt water gently into the eye for 10 minutes to remove the chemicals. If possible, the client's clothing should be protected with towels, or the head bent over a bowl or sink to catch the water. If sterile water is not available then use plain tap water either straight from the tap or by using a jug or similar container.

TIP BOX

It is not acceptable to use an eye bath for this procedure as large quantities of water are needed to flush the eye.

2 If the irritation does not cease after a good rinsing, the eye area should be carefully dried, covered with a sterile eye pad or a pad of clean non-fluffy material, and medical attention sought.

Foreign bodies in the eye

1 For a minor problem, e.g. an eyelash, proceed as in **1** above.

TIP BOX

Do not irrigate an eye with a wound or a foreign body lodged in or sticking to the eyeball.

2 If this does not work, the client must receive immediate medical aid. Further action could result in damage to the delicate conjunctiva covering the surface of the eye, possibly leading to permanent damage to the sight of the eye.

3 Do not attempt to remove a foreign body if it is at all stubborn. If it is on the pupil of the eye, embedded in the eyeball or cannot be seen (but the eye is inflamed and painful), you must not try to retrieve it yourself. Medical attention must be sought in such cases. Always err on the side of caution – the client's sight is at stake.

4 If medical attention is required, close the eyelid, cover with a large sterile eye pad extending on to the forehead and cheek, secure with a bandage, covering both eyes to prevent eye movement, and obtain medical aid.

Fainting

Fainting is a short period of lost consciousness caused by lack of blood flowing to the brain. It is frequently caused by an emotional or physical shock, e.g. ear piercing. It can also be caused by spending too long in a hot stuffy room, e.g. a sauna, a sunbed or an inadequately ventilated therapy room.

The casualty often gives good warning of an impending fainting attack:

- if standing they may sway, feel unsteady and dizzy
- the face may drain of colour, becoming a greenish white
- the casualty may sweat from the face, neck and hands.

● ● ● ● ● ● ● ● ● **FIRST AID** ● ● ● ● ● ● ● ● ●

1 If the casualty just feels faint, immediate action usually prevents a full faint occurring. Lay them down on the floor or a couch and raise their feet to stimulate blood flow to the head by placing pillows under their lower legs.

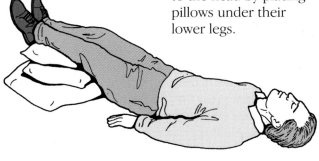

Alternatively, sit them down and bend them forward, placing the head between the knees as illustrated.

2 Loosen any tight clothing, reassure them and instruct them to breathe deeply. Open a window to supply fresh air if possible.

3 Instruct the casualty to flex the muscles of the thighs, buttocks and legs to stimulate the blood circulation.

4 If a full faint occurs, lay the casualty down as just instructed, loosen all tight clothing and, if there is any difficulty in breathing, place them in the recovery position (see page 114).

5 As the casualty recovers, they should be encouraged to gradually sit up. Check to see that they did not injure themselves while falling.

6 If the casualty does not regain consciousness quickly, check the breathing and pulse. Be prepared to resuscitate if necessary. Place them in the recovery position and send for an ambulance.

Falls

Falls are perhaps the commonest type of accident in the salon and often occur on staircases, in showers or on wet slippery floors. Whatever injury is sustained, a fall is always a rather startling and upsetting experience.

A fall can result in a variety of different types of injury. Bruises, sprains, strains and grazes are all common injuries, and can be very painful. In addition, the casualty may often knock their head as they fall. More severe falls can cause dislocated bones, fractures or deep cuts.

If the spine is twisted in any way, or the casualty is complaining of back or neck pain, or loss of sensation in their hands or feet, then under no circumstances must they be moved as it is possible that they have broken their spine. Movement in these cases could result in permanent paralysis. An ambulance must be summoned immediately and the casualty kept warm until it arrives.

TIP BOX

Anyone who suffers injury through a fall should receive a medical check-up. An injury which appears to the untrained eye as a sprain, may in fact turn out to be a break.

• • • • • • • • • FIRST AID • • • • • • • • •

See bruises, page 98; cuts, page 102; dislocations and fractures, page 104; grazes, below; sprains, page 115.

Finger and toe injuries

Injuries to fingers and toes are common, e.g. as a result of someone trapping a finger in a door, or from a weight accidentally dropped on to the foot. The injury will probably be very painful. Often there is internal bleeding, e.g. under the nail, although the skin is not broken.

• • • • • • • • • FIRST AID • • • • • • • • •

1 Apply a cold compress (see page 101) or put the injury under cold running water for at least 20 minutes to relieve the pain, reduce the swelling and stop the bleeding. Try to keep the injury elevated.

2 Advise the casualty to see their own doctor as soon as possible. If there is bleeding under the nail, the doctor will be able to puncture the nail to allow free bleeding, thus reducing pressure on the nail. If this is not done, the nail may be lost.

Grazes

Despite being minor wounds, grazes are usually very painful. They are shallow and therefore stimulate pain-sensitive nerve endings.

• • • • • • • • • FIRST AID • • • • • • • • •

1 Clean the wound by rinsing it lightly under running water. Using a cottonwool pad soaked in clean water, clean the area from the centre outwards so that infection is not taken into the wound. Use a clean pad, or area of pad, for each sweep.

2 If the injury is a simple small graze, pat it dry and apply a sterile gauze dressing or an adhesive dressing (plaster).

3 If the area is larger or contains dirt or grit, e.g. if the fall has been on the pavement outside your premises, then the graze needs to be cleaned and dressed by a doctor. The casualty will also need to be checked for tetanus immunity.

Headaches

Headaches can be caused by a variety of problems – too much heat or cold, illness, or even worry or stress. However, they may also be a symptom of something more severe, e.g. meningitis or stroke.

● ● ● ● ● ● ● ● ● **FIRST AID** ● ● ● ● ● ● ● ●

The sufferer must be reassured and helped to relax. If possible, they should sit or lie down in a quiet, well-aired, darkened room for a while, holding a cold compress (see page 101) against the forehead. If the headache persists for longer than two hours, call for medical help. If it recurs often, the casualty should be encouraged to consult their own doctor. Do not prescribe any internal medicines, e.g. aspirin or paracetamol. If the casualty requests a glass of water so that they can take their own medication, it is wise to check when and what was their last dose and what other medications are being taken, e.g. cold remedies, to avoid accidental overdosing (see below).

Paracetamol

No more than 1,000 mg of paracetamol can be taken in any one dose, and no more than 4,000 mg of paracetamol can be taken over a 24-hour period. More than this constitutes an overdose. An average tablet of paracetamol contains 500 mg of paracetamol. Bear in mind that other medications also contain paracetamol, e.g. Disprin and Lemsip. A paracetamol overdose is extremely dangerous because once it enters the bloodstream it does irreversible and often fatal damage to the liver.

Meningitis

One of the symptoms of meningitis is a headache. Other symptoms can include neck pain, back pain, flu-like aching all over the body, purplish blotches, rashes or pin-prick purple dots on the body, and visual problems, e.g. extreme sensitivity to light. If any of these symptoms accompany a headache, the casualty should be referred to a doctor immediately.

Heart attack

The main symptom of this is severe pain in the chest, often spreading to the left shoulder, arm and fingers, throat and jaws. Sometimes it spreads as far as the right arm too. The pain can also take the form of discomfort high in the abdomen, like severe indigestion. The pain will force the casualty to sit down or lean against something for support. Their skin colour can go ashen, with a blue tinge to the lips, and they may sweat. They may feel giddy or faint, sink to the ground, and go into shock. They will often become breathless, with a weak, irregular or rapid pulse, and may become unconscious.

● ● ● ● ● ● ● ● ● **FIRST AID** ● ● ● ● ● ● ● ●

This is aimed at reducing the work of the heart and sustaining the casualty until proper medical help arrives.

1 Do not move the casualty unnecessarily, but place them in a half-sitting, half-reclining position with their knees bent and supported, to make breathing easier.
2 Loosen clothing around the neck, chest and waist.
3 Call for an ambulance and tell them on the phone that you suspect a heart attack. If requested, call the casualty's doctor too.
4 Keep a continual check on the casualty's breathing and pulse rate. Be prepared to resuscitate if necessary.
5 If ordinary aspirin is available and the casualty is conscious, give them one tablet and tell them to chew it slowly. Inform the arriving medical staff that you have done this.

Heat exhaustion

Heat exhaustion is characterised by a rapidly developed high temperature and prostration caused by the body's inability to lose enough heat in very hot or humid conditions, e.g. a sauna or steam bath. Sudden movement by someone with heat exhaustion could result in them fainting, e.g. if they stand up quickly. Other symptoms may be headache, dizziness, nausea, sweating, cramps, a rapid and weak pulse, and shallow breathing.

● ● ● ● ● ● ● ● ● **FIRST AID** ● ● ● ● ● ● ● ●

1 Remove the casualty to cool surroundings to bring the temperature down. Encourage them to lie down at first with their legs supported and raised, to minimise the danger of fainting.

2 As they recover, administer sips of cold water. If cramps are present, it helps to add half a teaspoon of salt per litre of water.

3 The casualty should recover as they cool down. If they do not, medical aid must be summoned. Call for an ambulance.

4 If they lapse into unconsciousness, place them into the recovery position (see page 114). Record their pulse and breathing every 10 minutes until medical help arrives.

Infection control

Hepatitis B and HIV are the two infections which cause most concern for first-aiders.

Hepatitis B is a virus which causes inflammation of the liver. It is transmitted through contact with all body fluids, including blood and vomit. The virus can be absorbed through mucous membranes or it can enter the bloodstream through broken skin, e.g. piercing by a needle or other sharp instrument, grazes, cuts or skin diseases. Hepatitis C is another dangerous virus which is on the increase and is transmitted in the same way. If you think you need it, a safe vaccination against hepatitis B is available from your doctor.

HIV (human immunodeficiency virus) is the virus which causes AIDS (acquired immune deficiency syndrome). It needs direct contact between the carrier's blood or genital fluids and the recipient's bloodstream to cause infection. Entry can take place through broken skin.

A carrier is someone who is infected but has no symptoms. Many carriers do not know that they are harbouring disease. Both hepatitis B and HIV can be transmitted via a carrier.

Other blood-borne infectious diseases do exist, but if suitable precautions are being taken against hepatitis, you will be protected against these other diseases at the same time.

PROTECT YOURSELF

- Your skin is a natural barrier against infection entering your body. Therefore keep cuts, grazes and any broken areas covered with a waterproof dressing.
- Clean, waterproof rubber or plastic gloves should be worn when applying first aid to a casualty if any body fluids are involved.
- If no gloves are available, people who are bleeding can often be shown how to apply direct pressure and stop the bleeding for themselves. If this is not possible, the first-aider can use a plastic bag as an improvised glove, or use several dressings or other protective layers and apply direct pressure over these.
- If blood or other body fluids are spilled, pour sterilising fluid (half-strength Miltons 2 is recommended, and always wear gloves when using sterilising solutions) on to paper towels and place these over the spill. Pour more sterilising solution on the top. Throw the dirty towels into a yellow plastic rubbish bag which should be incinerated. Wipe up any remains and proceed to clean the area as normal.
- If a human bite or needle injury occurs, encourage bleeding by gently squeezing the wound then washing with warm soapy water. Advice should be sought from your own doctor or local hospital immediately.
- All laundry should be washed on a domestic hot-wash cycle.
- All sharp implements should be disposed of in a sharps disposal container (see page 47).
- After each procedure, wash your hands in hot soapy water. This applies even if gloves were worn.
- As a precaution, you should keep up your immunity to tetanus by having the applicable vaccination every 10 years. Hepatitis B vaccination is not essential for the low-risk occupations of hairdressing and beauty therapy, but further advice and vaccination can be obtained from your doctor if you think you are at all at risk.

Ingrowing hairs

If dead skin cells are allowed to collect over the follicle exit after a waxing treatment, the emergence of new, growing hair will be blocked, causing it to turn around and become ingrowing.

• • • • • • • • • **FIRST AID** • • • • • • • • •

1 Thorough moisturising after waxing or any other form of hair removal can help to avoid the problem. The client should be encouraged to buy and use one of the special aftercare moisturisers available for this purpose.

2 The client should be instructed to scrub the affected area thoroughly with a mildly abrasive appliance, e.g. a buff-puff, coarse massage sponge or a loofah, each time they shower or bathe, starting about 5–7 days after the waxing treatment. This will serve to remove the skin debris, thus leaving the follicle exit clear for the emergence of the new hair.

3 If the hair is already ingrown, it should be encouraged to come through the skin surface with a sterile needle. However, it should not be removed, but left in place so that the skin can heal to include a follicle exit in its structure. If it is removed, the skin will heal over completely and the ingrown hair will just recur.

4 If a client has a recurring and severe problem with ingrowing hairs, they should be discouraged from continuing with hair removal by the waxing method.

Inhalation of fumes

In the salon, this can be caused by the incorrect use of hairdressing chemicals such as bleach, strong cleaning and sterilising materials, acrylic nail liquids, fibreglass resin setting sprays, and the glues used with nail tips. Inhalation can result in dizziness or fainting.

• • • • • • • • • FIRST AID • • • • • • • • •

Remove the casualty to a well-ventilated area. Treat as a faint and encourage them to take deep breaths of fresh air. The quantities of solvent used in the salon should not present a serious problem and they should recover immediately.

Lice

If a client in the salon is discovered to be suffering from lice (and this discovery should take place no later than the initial combing through of the hair prior to shampooing), then the following procedures should be followed.

• • • • • • • • • FIRST AID • • • • • • • • •

1 The client should be quietly and courteously informed by a senior member of staff . They should not be made to feel ashamed – lice have no preference for clean or dirty hair.

2 The client should be told how to treat and eradicate the problem. It may be useful for the salon to have a printed help sheet containing this information and to supply lice combs, both

of which the client can take home with her (see point 6 below).

3 The client must leave the salon immediately to avoid passing on the infestation to others.

4 Every single item with which the client has been in contact must be thoroughly cleansed with a strong disinfectant or antibacterial solution. Small items which can be soaked. e.g. combs, towels, coathanger and gown, must be soaked in a strong disinfectant solution for no less than 20 minutes. Larger items, e.g. chairs, cubicle walls and floors, must be thoroughly washed down with a similar solution.

5 Members of staff who attended to the client must shower, scrub their nails, change their clothes, and treat their own hair in a way suitable for killing any infestation. The clothes which were worn while attending to the client must also be disinfected.

6 It is helpful for the long-term general control of lice to pass the following information on to the infested person, perhaps in the form of a handout. If the salon feels this is not possible for some reason, then the client should be told to go to her doctor or the chemist for further information and treatment advice.

Information for the client

Each louse takes 14 days to mature and be able to lay eggs. They live for up to 30 days and feed on blood sucked from the scalp, usually at night. Once mature they lay 6–8 eggs per day, gluing them in clusters to the hair shafts. The eggs take 7–10 days to hatch and the empty whitish egg cases are often known as nits.

Lice can be removed by using a fine-toothed louse comb made especially for this purpose. The eggs themselves are too small to be removed with the comb, but bearing in mind the life cycle of the louse, if the hair is thoroughly combed with a louse comb every day for two weeks to remove newly hatched lice before they lay eggs of their own, the cycle will be broken and the infestation eliminated. The easiest and most efficient way to do this is to shampoo and condition the hair first, combing with the louse comb while the conditioner is on the hair to make it easier for the fine-toothed comb to glide through the hair. Some authorities say doing this once every four days for two weeks is sufficient to eradicate an infestation.

After that, use of the louse comb once a week will prevent further infestation. This weekly maintenance combing is important in, for example, school children when there is an outbreak in the area. As well as this, regular normal combing and brushing of the hair damages lice so that they cannot cling on to the hair and so fall off and die.

The comb should be used in a logical pattern covering the whole of the head, parting the hair quickly into layers while looking for either moving lice or their eggs. Inspect and comb the whole head, paying particular attention to the nape of the neck, above the ears, and underneath the fringe. A towel or similar should be placed around the neck and shoulders to catch any debris while this procedure is being carried out. This towel can then be laundered on a hot cycle to kill any eggs or lice removed.

Insecticidal treatments can be used instead of the comb, but it should be noted that these, especially the alcohol-based lotion formulations, can trigger asthma or eczema attacks or cause headaches or a feeling of sickness. If already asthmatic or with a tendency to eczema, this should be explained to the doctor or pharmacist before a treatment product is either prescribed or bought so that they can supply a milder, water-based product more suitable for use by people prone to asthma or eczema. Insecticidal treatments such as these should not be used more than three times during the elimination of the lice.

There are three main types of insecticidal preparation – pyrethroids, carbaryl and malathion. The health authority rotates use of these every 2–3 years to prevent the lice from becoming resistant to them. Doctors and pharmacists know which one is in use at any one time, so these preparations should not be stored away for future use, but used up or disposed of, and new ones bought if the need should arise again at some future date.

Whichever way is chosen – insecticide or comb – all members of the family should be treated at the same time to avoid cross-infestation. The school attended, relatives, friends and anyone who has been in close contact over the last few months should be told, so that they too can check for infestation. This should not cause embarrassment because lice actually like to live in clean hair, so they are nothing to be ashamed about. Lice infect up to 5 million children alone in Great Britain every year.

Medical identification and treatment cards

If a person becomes unconscious for no apparent reason, call for an ambulance immediately and then search their clothes or purse for any form of medical identification while you are waiting for the ambulance to arrive. In this way, if a card is present, the ambulance personnel will be able to apply correct treatment straight away as the cause of the unconsciousness will be known.

Cards are issued for various reasons:

- An epilepsy card, usually issued by an epilepsy association, will confirm that the bearer has had fits in the past and that it is not a first-time occurrence.
- A diabetic identity card would explain dizziness, faintness or coma as being probably due to an excess of insulin in the body.
- An anti-coagulant card means that the bearer is taking drugs to reduce the clotting of blood and so is likely to bleed from a wound more than would normally be expected.
- A steroid card means that the bearer is undergoing some form of cortisone or other steroid treatment and is likely to collapse if placed in a stressful situation.

Medic-alert or SOS talisman bracelets, keyrings or necklaces are there to give any unusual medical particulars of the wearer, e.g. an unusual blood group. Sometimes they contain a phone number to ring for information about the casualty's medical history.

Other identification factors are:

- an insulin syringe (these can look like pens) and/or sugar lumps – these tell you that the casualty is a diabetic

TIP BOX

At an initial appointment, clients should be asked whether they suffer from any serious medical complaints, and a note entered on the personal record card. Gyms, solariums, beauty and alternative therapists should have a brief medical history of all their clients on their records.

- an inhaler – frequently carried by an asthmatic
- medicines – phenobarbitone or phenytoin are frequently carried by epileptics; glyceryl trinitrate for angina; indigestion tablets for a stomach ulcer.

Nail extension injuries

Injuries due to the wearing of artificial nails may occur after the client has left the salon. The nail technician must, therefore, be prepared to deal with injuries or complaints some time after the actual treatment took place.

• • • • • • • • FIRST AID • • • • • • • •

Cracks and splits

Cracks and splits in the natural nail plate are often due to the client neglecting their artificial nails so that they become loose at the base. If these are then caught and bent forward, the natural nail can split well below the flesh line and allow infection to enter the nail-bed area. If the client returns to you in this condition, the artificial nail must be removed and they must be sent to a doctor straight away.

Fungal infections

Fungal infections beneath artificial nails can occur due to lack of hygiene during application, or neglect during the wearing of the nails leading to 'lifted' areas which then provide an ideal habitat for fungal growth. Fungal infections cause the nail plate to discolour and turn black. Remove the artificial nail and refer the client to a doctor straight away with a covering letter. If left unchecked, the fungus can cause lifting of the natural nail plate.

Flaking and distortion

Severe flaking of the natural nail plate is common after the removal of artificial nails. The artificial nail acts as a barrier between the natural nail plate and the air, preventing any exchange of moisture, and causing the nail plate to dry out. Two or three good manicures, incorporating buffing and the use of a good nail cream or oil over the whole of the nail surface, should soon rectify this damage. Daily home use of such nail moisturising products will also help.

Distortion of the nail plate, e.g. a pin-tuck crease in the centre of the natural nail in the case of pre-formed plastic full false nails, or a narrowing of the free edge of the nail plate in the case of built-up extensions, cannot be avoided in clients whose natural nail shape predisposes them to this effect. In these cases, the client should be dissuaded from continuing to wear the artificial nails. The damage already caused in this way will then grow out as the natural nail grows forward.

Allergy

Allergy to artificial nail products sometimes occurs. Symptoms can include an eczematous reaction of the skin surrounding the nail or the face (through touching); a hot, unbearably itchy sensation around the nails; or the appearance of onychia (the lifting away of the natural nail plate from its bed). In cases like these the artificial nail product must be removed immediately and a doctor consulted to rectify any damage already done. Artificial nails of the same type should not be used on the client again, and a one-nail allergy test of any other product should be carried out before a different product is applied in the future.

If a member of staff becomes allergic to a product, they will not be able to work with that product again without suffering a recurrence of symptoms.

Nose bleeding

Nose bleeds can be caused by a blow, or may be spontaneous.

• • • • • • • • FIRST AID • • • • • • • •

1 Sit the casualty down with the head bent well forward. Loosen any clothing around the neck. They can sit in front of a sink, or use a large plastic bag containing tissues to catch the blood safely and effectively.
2 Ask the casualty to breathe through their mouth, then firmly pinch the soft part of their nose, to the front of the nasal bone (bridge), for about 10 minutes. If the bleeding has still not stopped, repeat this procedure.
3 If the bleeding does not stop after 30 minutes, the casualty must receive medical attention.
4 If it does stop, instruct the casualty to rest quietly for a few hours and not to blow their nose for at least four hours so that the clot is not disturbed. Also advise the casualty to see a doctor if the bleeding recurs.

Pulse rate

The heart is a strong muscular organ which contracts rhythmically to push blood around the body. Each thrust of blood creates a wave of pressure which can be felt or heard as the heart beat or pulse. In a normal healthy adult at rest, the rate varies from 60–80 beats per minute, the average being 72. In children the resting rate is higher, 90–140 beats per minute. In very fit adults it may be slower. The pulse rate may increase with exertion, fear, fever, blood loss and some illnesses. It may decrease with certain heart disorders, fainting or cerebral compression.

If the pulse rate needs to be taken (it is a useful check if you are worried about a person's condition in any way) count the rate for 30 seconds and double it to find the rate per minute. In this way there is less chance of error due to movement, and it is a much quicker process.

The pulse can be taken at various places throughout the body, but the three easiest areas are the neck, the wrist, and directly above the heart. The neck usually has the strongest and most easily felt pulse.

- **The neck**. Using the first and second fingers, feel for the pulse in the carotid artery just under the angle of the jaw in the hollow between the voice box and the adjoining muscle, approximately level with and below the corner of the mouth.

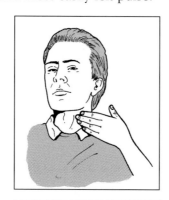

- **The wrist**. Using the first and second fingers, feel for the pulse about 1.5 cm in and down from the thumb side of the wrist.

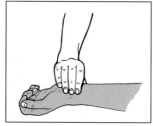

- **The chest**. Here the pulse can be felt directly over the apex of the heart, 5–8 cm above and slightly to the left of the base of the sternum.

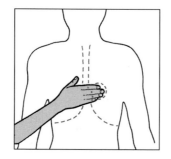

The thumb must never be used to take a pulse as it has a distinctive pulse of its own, which would serve to confuse the count of the casualty. The first two fingers are most often used for this process.

Recovery position

The recovery position is a comfortable and safe position in which to place an injured person while they recover consciousness or regain normal breathing.

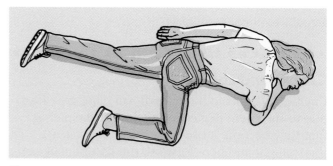

The recovery position

TIP BOX

Do not move a casualty whom you suspect may have injured their back or neck.

• • • • • • • • • **FIRST AID** • • • • • • • • •

1 Loosen any tight clothing and remove glasses if present.
2 Position the casualty on their back with their legs straight.
3 Tuck the hand nearest to you, arm straight and palm upwards, under the upper thigh. Make sure there are no breakable or bulky objects in their pockets.
4 Bring the far arm across the casualty's chest and hold the back of their hand against their cheek.
5 With the other hand, grasp the furthest thigh and pull the knee up while keeping the foot on the ground.
6 Keeping the casualty's hand pressed against their cheek with one hand, pull them towards you using the other hand on the upper leg.
7 Tilt the head back to maintain an open airway. Adjust the cheek hand so their head is well

supported and turned to the side to prevent choking.

8   The top leg should be bent at right angles to the body, the lower leg only slightly bent. Adjust the lower arm so the casualty is not lying on it and the palm is still facing upwards.

9   Check breathing and pulse regularly, at least every 10 minutes.

Shock

Shock can be caused by many things. In the salon, it is likely to be due to an emotional upset, e.g. brought on by ear piercing. Other causes would be heart attack, severe bleeding, or some other emergency situation. Shock can be recognised in the following ways:

• the face becomes pale and greyish in colour
• sweating, especially from the face and hands, occurs, but the skin feels cold and clammy
• the client may become dizzy and weak
• their breathing may become rapid and shallow, and their expression may become anxious and stunned
• there could be an initial increase in pulse rate, followed by a weak pulse which may appear to come and go.

• • • • • • • • • FIRST AID • • • • • • • • •

1   Reassure the casualty.

2   Make the casualty comfortable. Lie them down on the floor or a couch and raise their feet above their head. Loosen any tight clothing and cover with a blanket to keep warm. Do not apply direct heat, e.g. a hot water bottle, as this will draw the blood away from the body organs where it is needed. If the casualty is in any danger of being sick, place them in the recovery position or turn the head to one side.

3   Remedy the situation causing the shock. For example, if it is bleeding of some sort, stop the bleeding.

4   It is very doubtful if true shock would ever be experienced in the salon. The casualty should easily recover from minor emotional shock, e.g. from ear piercing. More severe cases, e.g. from electrocution or heart attack, need immediate medical attention and an ambulance should be summoned.

5   In severe cases, keep a record of pulse and respiration rate at least every 10 minutes to pass on to the medical help when it arrives.

Sprains

A sprain occurs at a joint. It is due to the wrenching or tearing of the ligaments and tissues connected with the joint.

The symptoms of a sprain are swelling at the joint, developing into bruising later on. If the person attempts to use the joint, increasing pain will be felt.

• • • • • • • • • FIRST AID • • • • • • • • •

1   Place the casualty in a comfortable position with the injury raised, supported and exposed.

2   Apply cold compresses (see page 101) in an effort to minimise swelling, bruising and pain.

3   Any pressure applied over the joint will help to ease the pain until the injury can be seen by a doctor. This can be done by surrounding the area with a good layer of cottonwool kept in place by a firm bandage, or the application of a firm crêpe bandage.

If you are in any doubt as to the severity of the injury, treat it as a fracture (see page 104).

Stings

If the sting has been inflicted by a bee, the sting, along with the poison sac, will be left in the skin. If you can see it, pull it out with tweezers, grasping the sting below the poison sac and as close to the skin as possible. **Do not squeeze the sting out**, as this only serves to spread the poison.

• • • • • • • • • FIRST AID • • • • • • • • •

For both bee and wasp stings:

1   Remove the sting as above.

2   Apply a cold compress (see page 101) straight away to relieve pain and minimise swelling.

3   Advise the casualty to see their own doctor if the pain and swelling continues or increases over the next two days.

If the sting is in the mouth, there is a great danger that swelling may interfere with breathing. Give the casualty ice to suck to minimise the swelling. Call for an ambulance and stay with the casualty, reassuring them, until help arrives.

Stitch

A stitch is a sharp pain in the upper abdomen caused by the diaphragm going into spasm. It is likely to happen to people in exercise classes who are unfit or who have eaten just before exercising.

● ● ● ● ● ● ● ● **FIRST AID** ● ● ● ● ● ● ● ●

Sitting down and resting should give relief within a few minutes. No other treatment is required. (See also cramp, page 102.)

Strains

A strain is the result of over-stretching a muscle, causing damage to the muscle or its tendon. The symptoms of a strain are a sudden sharp pain at the site of the injury, followed by possible swelling of the muscle and severe cramp. First-aid treatment is as for a sprain (see page 115).

Swallowing chemicals

Occasionally you may encounter an emergency in the salon where an inquisitive and restless child, for example, has swallowed a potentially harmful product. Chemicals frequently found in the hairdressing salon are shampoos, setting lotions, lacquers and treatment solutions. Chemicals frequently found in the beauty salon are surgical spirit, nail varnish remover and dilute antiseptic. Fortunately, all these, along with bleach, disinfectant, washing-up liquid, etc., are dealt with in the same way.

● ● ● ● ● ● ● ● **FIRST AID** ● ● ● ● ● ● ● ●

1 Do not cause vomiting. All the above substances are corrosive to a degree and will cause additional damage to the mucous membrane linings of the mouth and throat if regurgitated.
2 If the casualty's lips are burned by corrosive substances, give them frequent sips of cold water or milk to drink. This will cleanse the mouth, throat and oesophagus.
3 Find out exactly what was swallowed and, using your judgement as to the seriousness of the situation, if necessary arrange for the casualty to be taken directly to hospital along with a sample of the swallowed liquid.

Swellings and inflammation

Minor swellings and inflammation in the salon may be caused by eyebrow waxing or stings, etc.

● ● ● ● ● ● ● ● **FIRST AID** ● ● ● ● ● ● ● ●

1 Apply cold compresses (see page 101) as soon as any reaction occurs.
2 If the swelling does not subside completely, this could be due in part to an allergy. A doctor must be consulted immediately so that the correct treatment can be given. Antihistamines may be required.

Unconsciousness

This is due to an interruption of normal brain activity for some reason. The biggest dangers are from the loss of control of the muscles which normally keep the airway open, the loss of the cough reflex which normally keeps the throat clear of saliva, and possible regurgitation and inhalation of the stomach contents.

● ● ● ● ● ● ● ● **FIRST AID** ● ● ● ● ● ● ● ●

1 Lift the casualty's chin and tilt the head back to open the air passage. Check for breathing and pulse. Be prepared to resuscitate.
2 If the casualty has been in an accident or fall, assess and treat any serious injuries, e.g. punctured artery, but do not move them unnecessarily in case there is damage to the spine. Try to establish the cause of the unconsciousness. Are they carrying any medical identification? (See page 112.)
3 If it is safe to move the casualty, place them in the recovery position (see page 114).
4 If the casualty has been in an accident or does not regain consciousness within three minutes, send for an ambulance. Stay with them, recording pulse and breathing rates at least every 10 minutes, until the ambulance arrives.
5 If the casualty does regain consciousness within three minutes and is still well after 10 minutes, advise them to see their doctor.

Vaginal bleeding

This is most likely to be a severe menstrual bleed with accompanying cramps, but could also indicate miscarriage, recent abortion, or internal disease. If bleeding is severe, shock may develop.

● ● ● ● ● ● ● ● **FIRST AID** ● ● ● ● ● ● ● ●

1 Give the client some privacy to clean up, and the assistance of a female first-aider or chaperone.

2 Give her a sanitary pad or a clean towel.
3 Make her comfortable, with her upper body raised and supported and her knees bent up and supported to ease strain on the abdominal muscles.
4 If she knows that any pain is due to menstrual cramps, help her to take her own medication.
5 If bleeding is severe and continues, send for an ambulance and treat for shock (see page 115).

Waxing injuries

Waxing treatment can cause accidental removal of surface skin. This produces a red mark at first, which turns brown hours later and can take some weeks to fade. This can be very upsetting for the client. The hot wax may also cause burns and scalds.

Remember that ingrowing hairs may occur some time after treatment. You should know how to deal with them (see page 110).

• • • • • • • • • **FIRST AID** • • • • • • • •

Removal of surface skin

As heat has been used, treat as a burn (see page 99) and cool the area for 10 minutes. If the area affected is small, leave it open or cover with an adhesive dressing (plaster), depending on the severity. For a slightly larger area, apply a dry, sterile, non-fluffy dressing, followed by a crêpe bandage. If a large area is affected, apply the dressing and seek medical attention.

If, as the wax is gradually removed, the client shows any predisposition to the skin coming away, the treatment should be postponed to a later date and first-aid treatment applied to the affected area immediately. However, a reversal of the direction of pull to go *with* the direction of the hair growth instead of against it, and using a new, *clean* muslin strip for this action, can often remove residue wax while avoiding more skin from being removed

during an organic wax treatment. Obviously, the hair will not be removed either.

TIP BOX

If care is taken during a waxing treatment, serious problems should not happen. The treatment should be stopped at the first sign of skin removal occurring.

Wax scalds and burns

1 Thoroughly cool the area immediately for 10 minutes (see burns, page 99).
2 If the scald or burn is due to waxing and the wax is still on the client, leave the wax in place and cool for 10 minutes along with the rest of the area. You must not attempt to remove the wax. This is a job for the doctor to do, so that further damage to the skin is minimised.
3 Do not apply a dressing to an area coated in sticky wax as this will make it more difficult for the doctor to treat.

Winding

This can be caused by a blow to the upper part of the abdomen, e.g. in exercise classes where arms are being flung wide. It can cause fainting or even collapse.

• • • • • • • • • **FIRST AID** • • • • • • • •

1 Sit the casualty down.
2 Loosen any tight clothing at the chest and waist, e.g. shorts or waistbands.
3 Gently massage the upper abdomen.
4 When the casualty recovers, they should rest and not rejoin that particular exercise class.

PART FOUR

The legal requirements for the provision of first aid in the salon

The provision of first aid in the salon

It is the employer's responsibility to provide first-aid equipment and services for all their employees and clients in the event of an accident. The Revised Approved Code of Practice and Guidance on Health and Safety (First Aid) Regulations 1981, which came into force in 1996, stipulates the minimum requirements for first-aid provision at a place of work. These requirements vary according to the number of staff employed and the nature of the work carried out.

According to these regulations, hairdressing and beauty salons are workplaces where no special risk arises. They need only to provide an appointed person to assume responsibility during an emergency and at least one dustproof and waterproof first-aid box, well labelled with a white cross on a green background, containing a minimum of the items listed below.

First-aid box

FOR THE SALON

A salon first-aid box must contain the following items, by law:

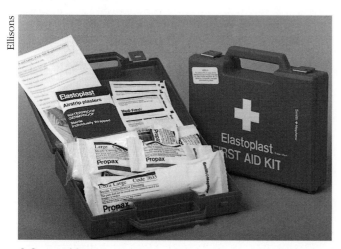

A first-aid box

- a guidance card (practical advice), e.g. HSE leaflet *First Aid at Work: General Guidance for Inclusion in First Aid Boxes*. This is available from Her Majesty's Stationery Office (HMSO) or booksellers. ISBN 0 11 883958 6
- 20 individually wrapped, sterile adhesive dressings (plasters) of assorted sizes
- 2 sterile eye pads, with attachments
- 6 individually wrapped triangular bandages
- 6 safety pins
- 6 medium-sized, individually wrapped, sterile, unmedicated wound dressings (approximately 10 cm × 8 cm)
- 2 large, sterile, individually wrapped, unmedicated wound dressings (approximately 13 cm × 9 cm)
- 3 extra large, sterile, individually wrapped, unmedicated wound dressings (approximately 28 cm × 17.5 cm).

Where tap water is not readily available for eye irrigation, sterile water or sterile normal saline in sealed disposable containers should be provided. Each container should hold at least 300 ml and at least 900 ml of such liquid should be provided.

The first-aid box should be easily accessible and situated if possible near to hand-washing facilities. Its contents should be checked regularly for deterioration and completeness by the person appointed to this task. It should be restocked immediately after use.

FOR MOBILE WORK

If outside work is done, e.g. home visiting or demonstrations given away from the premises, then a travelling first-aid box should be carried. Again, it should be dust and waterproof and marked with a white cross on a green background. It must contain a minimum of the following items:

- a guidance card (practical advice), e.g. the HSE leaflet *First Aid at Work: General Guidance for Inclusion in First Aid Boxes*

- 6 individually wrapped, sterile adhesive dressings (plasters) of assorted sizes
- 2 individually wrapped triangular bandages
- 2 safety pins
- 1 large, sterile, individually wrapped, unmedicated wound dressing
- 6 individually wrapped, moist cleansing wipes, e.g. non-alcohol Medi Wipes

TIP BOX

All mobile workers should consider buying a mobile phone to call for help if necessary.

RECOMMENDED ADDITIONAL ITEMS

Of course, all these requirements are a minimum. The following list of items are useful, but not legally necessary, additions to therapists' and hairdressers' first-aid equipment.

- A card giving the names, addresses and telephone numbers of local health centres, doctors, nurses, hospitals, fire stations, police stations and environmental health officers, and a list of the notifiable next of kin of each of the staff so that these can be contacted with the minimum of delay should the need arise
- individually wrapped moist cleansing wipes, e.g. non-alcohol Medi Wipes, for rapid cleansing of a damaged area
- a large washing-up bowl to hold water for cooling burns or splashing the eyes
- flexible waterproof plasters – keep more than stipulated as minor cuts are the most common type of injury in the salon
- a flexible cold compress pack to keep in a freezer, or a supply of ice
- disposable rubber or plastic gloves (non-seamed)
- paper towels for mopping up spills
- plastic bags for waste disposal or to use as gloves
- Miltons 2 sterilising solution to use at half strength to sterilise and clean up blood and body fluid spills
- an accident book for recording any accidents in the salon, reportable or not. A specially designed book is available cheaply from HMSO or all good booksellers and has the code number B1510.

Appointed persons

The salon environment is classed as a low-hazard workplace with under 50 employees. As such, it does not legally need a qualified first-aider on the premises. It does, however, need an appointed person present at all times.

An appointed person is someone who is authorised to take charge if a serious injury or illness occurs. They must be trained in how to take charge and telephone for help. A notice should be placed on the staff notice board informing everybody who the appointed person is, and stating that all first-aid treatments should be referred to them to be dealt with. In a salon, where small staff numbers, long and staggered working hours, holiday, pregnancy and sick leave, and time-consuming treatments often lead to irregular staff rotas and availability, it is advisable for all members of staff to be trained as appointed persons so that anyone available at the time of an emergency is able to assume charge if the one stipulated on the rota is not available.

The appointed person will be responsible for carrying out all first-aid treatments and follow-through procedures. They should record all accidents in an **accident book** (Form B1510, available from HMSO or any good booksellers), noting how, where and when the accident happened, the names and addresses of the clients and staff involved, and the first-aid procedure followed. If necessary, they (or their employers) must also report the incident to the necessary authorities (see Reporting of Injuries, Diseases and Dangerous Occurrences Regulations (RIDDOR) 1995, page 122).

If an incident is reportable under RIDDOR, additional records, e.g. the time the phone call was made to the Environmental Health Officer and the name of the person spoken to, additional casualty and accident details, and a copy of the accident report form (F2508), must also be kept.

It is also the appointed person's duty to replace any items used from the first-aid box as quickly as possible.

Although it is not legally necessary for an appointed person to possess any first-aid qualification, emergency first-aid training should be considered for all appointed persons. Various voluntary organisations run courses in first aid, in night-school or daytime format, and these are open to anyone who is interested. The three main organisations are St John Ambulance, The St Andrew's Ambulance Association, and The British Red Cross Society. Each of these organisations is listed in the telephone directory and will supply details of their courses on request.

Reporting of Injuries, Diseases and Dangerous Occurrences Regulations (RIDDOR) 1995

Reporting illness and accidents at work is a legal requirement. It enables the enforcing authorities (local environmental health officers are in charge of hair and beauty salons) to identify where and how risks arise and to investigate serious accidents. In this way, future injury and illness can be prevented.

- If there is an accident at work where anyone is killed or taken to hospital, the employer or appointed person must telephone the local Environmental Health Officer (EHO) as soon as possible. Within 10 days an accident report form (F2508) must be completed and sent to the local EHO.
- If there is an accident at work involving a staff member or self-employed person which does not necessitate a hospital visit but does result in the person being absent from work for more than three days (including non-working days), then the employer must send a completed accident report form (F2508) to the EHO.
- If an employee suffers from a reportable work-related disease as notified by a doctor, the employer must send a completed disease report form (F2508A) to the EHO. Such diseases include occupational dermatitis, occupational asthma and hepatitis.
- If an employee is in a car accident when on company business, this accident is reportable in the same way as an accident on the work premises. If, however, a single self-employed mobile worker is in a car accident going to or from a client, this does not need to be notified.
- Accidents as a result of violence or attacks need only be reported if serious physical injury is sustained.
- If you are self-employed and suffer a reportable injury while working on someone else's premises (e.g. a rent-a-chair situation), the owner of the premises is responsible for reporting the accident, so you must make sure that the owner knows about the accident and reports it by both telephone and accident report form (F2508) if applicable.
- If you are working on your own premises and suffer an accident, or there is a dangerous occurrence, or a doctor tells you that you are suffering from a reportable disease, you do not have to report it by telephone immediately. Allowance is made for the fact that you may be incapable of doing this at the time. However, either you or someone acting for you should send in an accident report form (F2508) within 10 days.
- A dangerous occurrence is one that could have resulted in a reportable injury but didn't, e.g. a ceiling collapsing at night when the premises are empty. The incident must be reported by telephone to the EHO as soon as possible. Send a completed accident report form (F2508) to the EHO within 10 days.
- If you are a mobile worker working in someone's home at the time of a reportable accident to yourself, or which you have inflicted on the client, it is your duty to report this to the EHO immediately by telephone. Send a completed accident report form (F2508) to the local EHO within 10 days.

A full list of reportable major injuries, diseases and dangerous occurrences is included with the accident report forms (F2508) and in the guide to the regulations, or you can simply telephone your nearest HSE to find out further details.

TIP BOX

A booklet, *Everyone's guide to RIDDOR '95* (ISBN 0 7176 1077 2) is available free from the HSE. (Your local Environmental Health Officer may have spare copies to give away.) It contains lists of definitions of major injuries, diseases and dangerous occurrences which need to be reported and a copy of the accident report form F2508. All HSE publications are available from HSE Books, PO Box 1999, Sudbury, Suffolk CO10 6FS. Telephone 01787 881165.

What an employer must do in the event of an accident at work

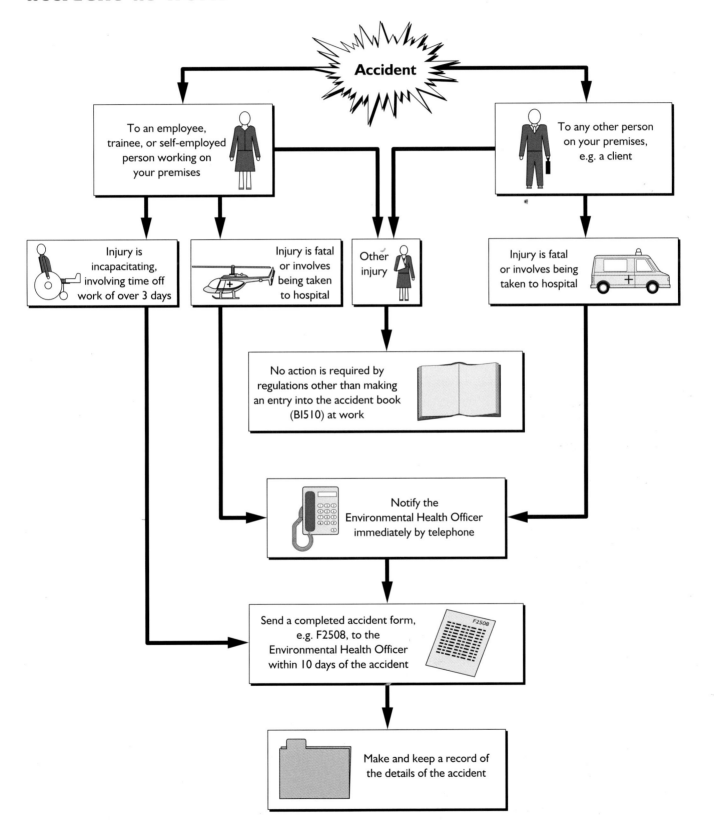

The Health and Safety at Work Act 1974

COSHH The Control of Substances Hazardous to Health Regulations 1994	PPE Personal Protective Equipment at Work Regulations 1992	Workplace (Health, Safety and Welfare) Regulations 1992	Health and Safety (Display Screen Equipment) Regulations 1992	Manual Handling Operations Regulations 1992
Set out the required handling and usage of hazardous substances in the workplace. They demand that a written risk assessment of all products be made	Require that unavoidable hazardous substances, equipment and treatments be identified and suitable protective equipment be supplied for use where necessary	State the legal requirements for maintaining a safe, secure working environment with regards to ventilation, lighting, temperature, maintenance of the workplace and equipment, cleanliness, waste disposal, toilets, staff facilities for eating, resting, drinking, clothing, washing, safe salon planning, layout, seating, workstations, etc.	Set out the rules regarding computer operation, e.g. seating, working heights, rest periods, screen emissions, etc.	Applicable where manual lifting occurs, they require risk assessments of any lifting activities and action to be taken to minimise any risks
See page 24	See page 39			

PUWER Provision and Use of Work Equipment Regulations 1992	Electricity at Work Regulations 1989	RIDDOR Reporting of Injuries, Diseases and Dangerous Occurrences Regulations 1995	RISK The Management of Health and Safety at Work Regulations 1992	Gas Safety Regulations 1994
Affecting both new and old equipment, these stipulate health and safety controls regarding the provision and use of equipment, selection, maintenance, training, manufacturers' information, dangers of injury, and the duties of the owners and users	State that electrical equipment must be adequately maintained and checked by qualified people and a written record of the checks kept for inspection	Cover the reporting and recording of certain serious accidents and conditions to the relevant authorities	Require that an assessment be made of *any* risks to the health and safety of *any* person in the workplace. This assessment should show that all risks have been considered, then eliminated, controlled or minimised.	State that gas equipment must be adequately maintained and checked by Corgi-registered gas engineers and a written record of the checks kept for inspection
	See page 26	See page 122	See page 43	See page 32

APPENDIX 2

List of abbreviations

AIDS   acquired immune deficiency syndrome
BSIA   British Security Industry Association
CIT   cash in transit
COSHH   Control of Substances Harmful to Health
CPO   Crime Prevention Officer
CPR   cardio-pulmonary resuscitation
EC   European Community
EHO   Environmental Health Officer
FPO   Fire Prevention Officer
HIV   human immunodeficiency virus
HMSO   Her Majesty's Stationery Office
HSE   Health and Safety Executive
ISBN   international standard book number
NACOSS   National Approval Council for Security
            Systems
PPE   personal protective equipment
RIDDOR   Reporting of Injuries, Diseases and
            Dangerous Occurrences Regulations
RSI   repetitive strain injury
TST   total sterilisation test
VDU   visual display unit

INDEX